LEAVING ABUSIVE PARTNERS

LEAVING ABUSIVE PARTNERS

From the Scars of Survival to the Wisdom for Change

Catherine Kirkwood

SAGE Publications
London • Thousand Oaks • New Delhi

First published 1993
Reprinted 1995, 1997

SAGE Publications Ltd
6 Bonhill Street
London EC2A 4PU

SAGE Publications Inc
2455 Teller Road
Thousand Oaks, California 91320

SAGE Publications India Pvt Ltd
32, M-Block Market
Greater Kailash – I
New Delhi 110 048

British Library Cataloguing in Publication Data

Kirkwood, Catherine
  Leaving Abusive Partners: From the Scars
  of Survival to the Wisdom of Change
  I. Title
  362.82

ISBN 0–8039–8685–8
ISBN 0–8039–8686–6 (pbk)

Library of Congress catalog card number 93–084704

Typeset by Megaron, Cardiff, South Wales
Printed and bound in Great Britain by
Biddles Ltd, Guildford and King's Lynn

This book is dedicated to the women who shared their wisdom with me and to every woman who finds the courage to transform her experience of abuse into vision that enlightens all our paths.

Contents

Acknowledgements

This book could not have been produced without the contributions of a number of people. Foremost of these were the women who agreed to be interviewed about highly intimate and painful experiences in their lives. They offered wisdom which not only served as a foundation for what is written here, but also ultimately comprised what I now recognize as a great personal gift to myself. The truth they spoke, in many different styles and words, fuelled the commitment I held to completing this work. I also thank the organizations, both in England and in the US, which helped me contact these women and whose staff offered valuable insight and advice about how to sensitively conduct this study.

In addition, I could not have offered such clarity of thought and analysis if it had not been for the hours of conversation and support of Mary Maynard, or the enlightening and revitalizing observations offered by Carol-Ann Hopper, Liz Kelly and my editor, Karen Phillips. I also want to thank the staff and students of the Centre for Women's Studies, University of York, who continually stood by me in my struggles and successes. Thanks are also due to Sue Baxter, whose enthusiasm vitally re-energized my motivation at the most needed times.

Special thanks are due to my parents, Patricia and Robert, and my brothers, John and Robert, who were eternally convinced of my abilities to succeed and who offered enormous and unquestioned financial support towards the completion of this study.

I am grateful to Shona M.G. Philp who, in addition to her unflagging dedication to proof reading, resolution of computer problems, and copious word processing, saw me through the daily experience of research and writing this book – my excitement, fear, frustration and sadness about the topic I studied. Thanks too go to Jess and Freyja, who reminded me that there's more to life than work.

Introduction

The last two and a half decades of research into 'battered women' have produced a wealth of information and theory about why such abuse occurs, using social, psychological, historical and political perspectives. The surge of interest was sparked by social changes, created by feminists, towards public acknowledgement of the problem and the establishment of services for women seeking to leave violent men. The existing research and literature describe the degree, extent and dynamics of violence and offer explanations as to why abuse occurs. They include theories about the psychology of 'battered women', social factors which support violence in the family, and political perspectives on the relationship between violence and male domination over women. Women's experience of abuse extends past the ending of their relationships with abusers and colours their struggle to maintain independent lives. However, there is more to the story of 'battered women' than their experiences with violence and the relationship in which violence is enacted.

This book is intended to extend and build upon feminist work by exploring women's experiences after leaving their partners. I demonstrate that formerly abused women face a number of emotional, material and social problems. These include their processes of healing from and coping with the lasting emotional impact of abuse. Recovering from the impact of emotional abuse is central to women's experiences after they had left their relationships. In addition, the women interviewed faced material problems in maintaining independence and in the negative responses from and beliefs held by others about their experiences of abuse. Women's subjective experiences of these problems, which often compound and reinforce the emotional issues they face, reveal that 'leaving an abuser' is a process which is achieved through many different strategies, extending far past the ending of a relationship with an abuser. The way in which women engage in this process contributes to their 'survival', a term which I argue can be applied to a multi-dimensional struggle to become free from abuse and its impact.

In Chapter 1, I review some of the most significant and illustrative contributions to the extensive body of mainstream research on 'battered women'. This research falls into two categories: psychological literature and conventional sociological literature. In each section I follow the development of thought in these disciplines which is relevant to my study and point to gaps in our knowledge. I also highlight where each area contributed to current debate and criticism concerning theories on woman abuse from which I draw in the analysis of the experiences of the women I interviewed.

In Chapter 2, I look at the challenges feminism has made in response to traditional work. I then draw upon both traditional and feminist methodology to describe and support the techniques I employed in my own research.

In Chapters 3 and 4, I explore the notion of emotional abuse. Chapter 3 focuses on the elements and nature of emotional abuse. Chapter 4 demonstrates the relationship between emotional abuse, the emotional impact of physical abuse and the dynamics of power and control in the women's relationships with abusers. It also discusses how women act to shift the imbalance of power such that they are able to leave their partners.

In Chapter 5, I discuss women's experiences of meeting their material needs after leaving abusers, including information, housing, money, medical aid and protection. Chapter 6 reveals that the emotional impact of abuse and leaving an abuser has both a short-term and a long-term effect on the lives of formerly abused women. It explores the nature of this effect and how women cope with it. This is followed by an exploration of women's experiences of the negative responses and views held by others about abuse and of the representations of 'battered women' they see in the media, as well as how women's experiences of this after their relationships end may compound and reinforce the impact of the abuse from which they suffer.

In Chapter 7, I argue that the concepts of both victimization and survival are important to women's own understanding and expression of their experiences. Moreover, the latter concept is used by women to express how they cope with and overcome issues confronted after leaving their abusers. In this light, I assert that the term 'survival' applies to three dimensions of women's action for personal and social change and is useful in understanding how women transform their past experiences into positive opportunities for healing and growth.

In conclusion, I draw together the conceptual and empirical insights of my study to look at how we might reframe the concept of 'battered women' to include the many dimensions of their journeys towards surviving abuse.

1
The Face of a 'Battered Woman': Traditional Approaches to Understanding Woman Abuse

In December 1988 one of the most famous trials concerning a 'battered woman' was splashed across the headlines. Despite two and a half decades of research, media interest and political action, the face of a battered woman still held the intrigue and mystique necessary to sell issues of papers and journals. Hedda Nussbaum had been beaten and emotionally abused by her partner Joel Steinberg over a period of years. When one day he battered their adopted child, Lisa, Nussbaum did not telephone the emergency services which might have saved her daughter's life. The questions as to why she did not, whether she was psychologically able to assume this responsibility after years of abuse, and how such personal devastation might have occurred became the subject of extensive media investigation. Many of these reports consisted of disjointed arrays of psychological and social factors which 'experts' insisted contributed to Nussbaum's experience.

What is significant about this court case and the public interest that surrounded it is that it reveals the divergent strands of understanding which have developed over the last 25 years and which have fuelled, and been fuelled by, an enormous body of research on 'battered women' or 'domestic violence'. The portrayal of Nussbaum reflects the diversity and debate between and within these strands. In fact, it illustrates the development and current state of knowledge more coherently than it presents a description of what happened to Hedda Nussbaum. Thus, it provided a starting point for tracing some major findings of research.

The issue of a mother's care or lack of care for a dying child engenders strong public reaction which is also apparent in the emotive tone taken in some of the reports of the case. For the purposes of this work, what is of interest is not how the court case was resolved, not whether Nussbaum could or should have phoned the emergency services, but rather the manner in which the public is informed about abuse and how this is rooted in a history of hotly debated research.

The body of existing research is enormous and, since it is not possible to describe in detail all of this work, I will focus on the key research which represents the major perspectives. The two sections of this chapter – on psychological and sociological research – draw almost entirely upon academic studies concerning physical violence and the behaviour or experience of women within relationships with violent men. Feminist perspectives, which critically draw on both sociological and psychological disciplines but also demonstrate how knowledge about battered women has been further extended from an interrelated development of both research and a social movement, will be addressed in Chapter 2.[1] These are presented separately from others as they provide a framework for understanding different approaches to explaining abuse which is relevant to the conclusions drawn in this book.

The article I have chosen, as an example of how research is presented in popular accounts, was published in *Newsweek* on 12 December 1988, in the U.S. Edition, and was probably one of the more widely consulted reportings of the case. *Newsweek* is a news reporting journal widely read in both the US and the UK;[2] it offered a headline story of the Steinberg trial and a cover story in the US edition, and could be seen to represent a source of information from which many people may have sought to understand what was occurring. It also reflects many of the issues present in other articles and thus serves as a useful distillation of media portrayals.[3] As such it provides a link between what the public may have come to understand about woman abuse from reading about Hedda Nussbaum in a widely circulated report in a respected news journal, and the vast body of research on this topic to which most readers would not have access. My intention is both to review the research – its development, flaws and contributions to knowledge – and to illustrate how its results have been translated from academic into popular perspectives on woman abuse.

The Psychology of 'Battered Women'

Nussbaum's first day of testimony ended with the image of a helpless and innocent child, lying comatose on a bathroom floor while her parents ignored her and freebased cocaine. (*Newsweek*, 12 December 1988: 56)

Even though the girl remained unconscious, with water and undigested food oozing out of her mouth, Nussbaum did little more than ineffectually pump the girl's chest and occasionally check her pulse. (p. 58)

One of the more puzzling aspects of Nussbaum's testimony supports the notion that a battered woman can harbor tenderness toward a child while simultaneously neglecting her. During her inadequate efforts to save Lisa, Nussbaum removed and washed the girl's soiled underpants, and wrapped her in a blanket . . . Nussbaum also said that during the hours Lisa lay comatose, she consulted medical dictionaries in an effort to find out what was wrong with her. (pp. 58–60)

A number of contrasting descriptions of Nussbaum, her actions, and the impact of abuse on women in general are offered within the *Newsweek* article. Together, they reflect the diverse perspectives of the psychology of abuse and battered women. In the article, as the passages above illustrate, such perspectives are not explicitly distinguished and are presented as an incoherent, internally confusing and contradictory description of Nussbaum.

In the above passages, Nussbaum ignores her dying child; is mildly although ineffectively active in her attempts to save Lisa; and is extremely active, tender and caring in response to the crisis she faced. This first set of three quotes is stunningly contradictory, particularly as it is drawn from the main body of the article that was only a few pages long. With this portrayal, is it any wonder that it is difficult to understand why Nussbaum behaved the way she did? Yet if we look more closely at what is being said, we can see the unmistakable vestiges of research that has been said to 'explain' the issue of 'battered women'.

Initially Nussbaum is described as totally in control of her circumstances, choosing to 'ignore' her dying daughter. Because it is difficult to imagine having this response to a dying and badly beaten child, this representation implies she was, in some way, psychologically deviant. When read with the following quote a fuller picture of this construction arises. *Newsweek* reports that, as the court case progressed, 'attention turned to the dynamics of the perverse relationship between the two adults' (p. 58). Here Nussbaum is an equal partner in creating a relationship with perverse dynamics. The image is created of two adults who enter into and willingly maintain a relationship in which one is severely abused and the other is capable of life threatening violence. In this particular analysis, offset by the image of a powerless dying child, there is no room for speculation about who ensures that the dynamics are preserved and how, and about what impact such dynamics have on the other who copes and survives. In short, they are both implicated in the 'perversity' of their relationship. This approach underlies much of the earliest psychological research on 'battered women' which saw them as masochists, emotionally deviant in so far as they sought out violent partners in order to fulfil their own distorted psychological needs.

The second extract depicts Nussbaum as being ineffective and somewhat passive in her attempts to save the child, although clearly her actions demonstrate that she was concerned and not ignoring the problem. In addition to this passage, she is also quoted as saying that she believed Steinberg when he told her he would heal their daughter, clearly demonstrating concern for the child if also a somewhat distorted view of Steinberg's capabilities. These coupled with the following passages indicate an awareness that Nussbaum was incapacitated by the effects of abuse:

> She was a slave, totally submissive to this man, with no ability or will to save her daughter. (p. 60)

> Nussbaum might have saved Lisa with a phone call. But she didn't for fear of angering the man she loved, the man who left her with a fighter's face. (p. 59)

According to these representations, her will and abilities were destroyed by her fear of Steinberg's violence. She was a complete victim to his beliefs and abuse. This reflects a second strand of understanding which developed in response to the blaming perspective that battered women are masochists, and, clearly from the quotes above, it is another dimension of the perplexing image of battered women offered by popular accounts.

Yet, there is a hint in the language of a third perspective. Steinberg left Nussbaum with a 'fighter's face'. Along with reference to the severe physical injuries and scars visible on Nussbaum's face, this terminology also speaks of Nussbaum as a fighter. Within the final extract opening this section, it is clear that Nussbaum *was* fighting to save her daughter's life. She kept Lisa warm and clean, and consulted the only expertise which she felt was safe – medical dictionaries. Moreover, an executive medical director of the hospital in which she was recovering asserted that 'Nussbaum's gradual acceptance of Steinberg as a godlike figure follows an established pattern. "People wonder how someone can tolerate a situation and not walk out," he says, "it's like what happens to someone in a concentration camp. They are reduced, by virtue of physical torture, to a mere existence level. They shut off normal human emotions" ' (p. 61). Within this perspective, then, she battled with conditions comparable to concentration camps, in which emotions must be damped or shut off in order to survive. In this view, rather than a submissive victim or a perverse masochist, she is a fighter within the most adverse psychological conditions, and she is a survivor of the traumatic and painful death of her child. This is a final strand of psychological approaches. It investigates the experience of abuse from the perspective of women without minimizing the action they take to cope with, stay alive in a relationships with, and leave abusers.

Three perspectives within psychological thought – abused women as masochists, victims and survivors – are extremely significant because they are still present in popular writing about abuse. Furthermore, a study of the last 25 years of literature shows them as markers of the stages of development in psychological research on the topic. As we will see later in this chapter, these psychological approaches to understanding 'wife battering' were among the first to develop, and thus provided a primary foundation of knowledge which has been drawn upon in later research and debate within other disciplines. Also, these three foci influence how abused women perceive how others view them (see Chapter 6) and the ways in which they understand their own experience of abuse (see Chapter 7).

Specifically, early research discussed in this section is composed of investigations into the ways in which individual couples relate, the personality characteristics of both 'battered women' and battering men, and the psychoanalytical reasons for these behaviours and characteristics. Subject populations were drawn almost exclusively from clients of psychological or psychiatric treatment. Focus on individual behaviour and personality within professional treatment produced a perspective in which both the husband and the wife were seen as deviant, and solutions addressed the different methods of therapy.[4] Later analyses challenged these assumptions about 'battered women's' deviancy and the other concepts addressed in this chapter.

'Perverse Relationships': a Study in Female Masochism
The first perspective on battering in marriage to arise from psychological studies offered explanations which focused on extreme female masochism and psychological deviance displayed by battered women. Elizabeth Pleck (1987) has suggested that the legacy of Freud influenced the predominant psychological theories held about women in the 1960s. Pleck observed that Freud attributed the phenomenon of incest to the imagination of his female patients who reported memories of sexual abuse. From this premise, Freud developed the theory that women unconsciously wish to engage in sexual behaviour with their fathers, and thus create fantasies as adults to fulfil this need. By describing reported incest as a result of the insufficient psychological development of women, Freud initiated the creation of the image of the masochistic woman. Pleck concluded that it was this image, developed by Freud, which re-emerged in the first discussions of battered women in the 1960s. Pleck cites Deutsch and Horney as the first psychoanalysts to apply the masochism theory to battered women or women who have been raped (Pleck, 1987).

Illustrations of this general trend can be found in the work of John Snell et al. from the US and Pizzey and Gayford in the UK, but can also be found in other studies (Gayford, 1975; 1976; Koslof, 1984; Loseke and Cahill, 1984; Mazzola, 1987; Millman, 1975; Morgan, 1981; Scott, 1974; Snell et al., 1964; Waites, 1977; Weitzman and Dreen, 1982) and is acknowledged in more recent critiques (Pizzey and Shapiro, 1981; Pleck, 1987; Shainess, 1977). Snell et al.'s (1964) analysis typifies the stereotype of battering couples depicted by American psychiatrists in the 1960s. Their conclusions were consistent with Freudian terminology:

The periods of violent behavior by the husband served to release him momentarily from his anxiety about his ineffectiveness as a man, while, at the same time, giving his wife apparent masochistic gratification and helping probably to deal with the guilt arising from the intense hostility expressed in her controlling, castrating behavior. (p. 111)

The researchers asserted that the dual dependency and deviance exhibited by the 'battering couple' exposed wife battering as a method employed by the couple to maintain an equilibrium. This equilibrium, according to Snell et al., allowed couples to continue to express their maladjusted personality traits, and produced a situation in which behavioural change was unlikely. Thus the masochistic woman was as much to blame for the violence enacted upon her as her equally deviant husband.

This perspective is also found, but does not seem as blatant, in psychological analyses of the 1970s and 1980s. Although Freudian terminology diminished in popularity, like Snell et al's theory, battering was viewed as a result of abnormality in female psychology, but more emphasis was placed on the unconscious nature of women's masochism.

For example, in 1975, British psychiatrist J.J. Gayford published a survey of 100 battered wives residing in refuges. The women cited many practical and economic reasons for staying in their relationships and illustrated the severity of emotional trauma experienced by women through data on suicide attempts (Gayford, 1975). Despite this, Gayford's main focus was placed on personal background factors such as whether the women had had sex before marriage, had had affairs, or had been pregnant by men other than their husbands. Without a comparison to the response of women in non-violent relationships, he concluded that battering is correlated with characteristics such as sexual promiscuity (Gayford, 1975). Thus he constructed a profile of battered women which included a multitude of behaviours that were considered culturally deviant for women, and in doing so suggested that these were causal factors in abuse.

Gayford's work was popularized and backed up by Erin Pizzey (1974), founder of the first women's refuge. Because of the accessibility of their work, Gayford and Pizzey became the most well known 'experts' on battered women in the early and mid 1970s and their conclusions formed a basis of popular British understanding of battered women for a number of years. In addition to the criticisms already forwarded, the work of Pizzey and Gayford is questionable with regard to what degree it was generalizable. Both researchers based their analyses on the psychological condition of women living in refuges, in particular Chiswick Women's Aid. Overcrowding, and the often poor living conditions, were particularly problematic in refuges set up early in the movement (NWAF, 1977). This, combined with a woman's fear of her husband's wrath and the practical obstacles of living without him (NWAF, 1977; Pahl, 1985a; 1985b), may have contributed to a temporary psychological state of trauma during the period in which the women were studied. It is not clear whether either Pizzey or Gayford attempted to distinguish between the psychological traits exhibited as a reaction to coping with shelter life and those attributed to masochism in individual personalities.

The masochistic theory generated studies which, in response, have questioned the stereotype of battered women. For example, Beck et al. (1982) conducted a comparative study of battered and non-battered women in a psychiatric hospital. They concluded that battered women who have been institutionalized for psychological disorders did not possess more self-destructive, or 'masochistic', personalities than women in the same psychological condition who had not been in violent relationships. Thus it is unlikely that 'masochism' is a psychological characteristic specific to battered women.

From Masochist to Victim
In the mid to late 1970s a variation on the theme of masochism became dominant. The image of battered women as victims disguised the way in which blame for the violence was placed on the woman who stayed with her batterer. Sociological studies have contributed to this perspective by revealing that the extent and severity of violence is so extreme that an explanation based solely on individual female deviance seems insufficient. Also, studies showing that women rarely provoked assaults and could do little to prevent them seemed to challenge explanations based on female masochism. These introduced an image of battered women as victimized and helpless at the hands of brutal or insane husbands (Claerhout et al., 1982; Jackson and Rushton, 1982; Lion, 1977; Marin, 1985; Marsden and Owens, 1975; Walker, 1979a; 1979b; 1984).

In accordance with this perspective, *Newsweek* reports that Nussbaum was a 'slave, totally submissive to this man with no ability or will to save her own daughter'. Despite, as I have noted above, the reports of her actions to save Lisa, albeit unsuccessful, the image of Nussbaum as utterly destroyed in will and ability to act is extremely strong in this passage. The message here is that, rather than being an adult equally responsible for maintaining a perverse relationship, she is completely incapacitated by the abuse she has experienced. She is passive and submissive because the abuse has rendered her psychologically unable to fight and act in her own behalf. So what is the evidence that supports *this* potent and strikingly different protrayal of an abused woman?

Lenore Walker's theory of 'learned helplessness' is particularly illustrative of the psychological focus on the victim stereotype. Walker published an extremely popular American book on wife beating in 1979. In the genre of American self-help books, Walker explained in simple terminology the dynamics of an abusive relationship. From hundreds of case studies she described a 'cycle of violence' to which battered women are subjected. In this cycle, women experience a stage of mounting tension in their partners over which they have little control, followed by violent assaults, and finally a stage of apology and contrition expressed by their batterers. Walker proposed that this cycle 'taught' women to be helpless and passive.[5]

She proposed that the common characteristics of battered women might have been more accurately seen as a result rather than a cause of battering: 'They do not choose to be battered because of some personality deficit but develop behavioral disturbances because of the battering' (Walker, 1979a: 168–9). This perspective has been supported by others (Prescott and Letko, 1977). Thus it became clear, with the development of research on battered women, that the characteristics described as 'deviant' in the late 1960s and early 1970s may more accurately have been described as common responses to severe and continuous abuse.

Although this insight moved psychological analyses on battered women forward and allowed the growth of new perspectives to counter masochism theories, it also introduced the idea that battered women were helpless. This image has been challenged since Walker published her work. For example, the formation of the victim image has been called 'victimism' (Barry, 1979), and has been said merely to offer a new stereotype of women which ignores the power they do have over their own lives. Thus Walker, in providing one of the most widely known works about the impact of abuse on women's behaviour, did not challenge the basic premise that women who were repeatedly battered suffered from psychological abnormalities. Neither did she question the view that battered women were in need of psychological retraining and interventive aid from external agencies or professionals as suggested by the 'masochism theory'. In both cases emphasis was placed on individual personality problems, implying that some responsibility lay with the women. This, in turn, suggested that the solution lay in changing the behaviour of battered women. In this respect, Walker's analysis seems appropriate to her source of knowledge: individual therapeutic work with battered women. As later studies have shown, this perspective is an insufficient approach to understanding the complex psychological dynamics of women battering.

A 'Fighter's Face': from Victim to Survivor
In the 1980s American and British psychological researchers and therapists produced studies which showed that a woman was not a

passive victim of either her own 'masochistic psychology' or the psychological stresses, such as fear and hopelessness, produced by the abuse. Allusions to this are present in the *Newsweek* article. In addition to using the perhaps inadvertent but appropriate phrase 'a fighter's face', *Newsweek* reported Nussbaum's active attempts to save Lisa. It also noted that she attempted to leave several times. This suggests that Nussbaum was *not* without a will of her own, nor was she totally submissive. Rather she seems to have been recurrently testing out new ways of maintaining her own life and that of her child, balancing her actions in order to preserve her safety from a man who was extremely violent and whose abuse had led her to perceive him as immensely more powerful than she.

This third image of an abused woman's psychology can be traced to studies which revealed that battered women constantly re-evaluated their situation and opportunities for change. These studies revealed that the psychological aspects of woman battering included far more than individual personality characteristics. For example, reactions of women to the abuse and to the external society that stigmatized or ignored abuse were significant to the psychological understanding of battered women. The studies described here are feminist in that they challenge other approaches by understanding abuse through the framework of women's perspectives and include recognition of gender socialization as a factor contributing to abuse. They are included in this section because they developed as a direct response to the studies previously described in this chapter.

Ferraro and Johnson (1983), for example, reported on the psychological mechanisms used by battered women which allowed them to understand and emotionally cope with the violent environment in which they lived, as well as on the psychological processes that resulted in their decision to leave. Ferraro and Johnson named six types of 'rationalization' used by women who return: 'the appeal to salvation ethic' in which women used their role as nurturers to justify staying with a man who needed psychological help; 'the denial of the victimizer' in which women did not perceive their batterers' use of violence as a form of abuse; 'the denial of injury' in which battered women minimized or trivialized the extent of physical or emotional injury they suffered; 'the denial of victimization' in which women did not see themselves as being abused; 'the denial of options' in which women asserted that they had no other option but to stay with their partners; and 'the appeal to higher loyalties' (either traditional or religious) in which women felt they could not leave because social or religious ethics demanded that they stay with their partner. As evident in other literature, these findings can be analysed in different ways. Linda Gordon (1986) described the first type of rationalization, 'the appeal to the salvation ethic', as part of the victimization of women by a cultural ideology which imposed the role of nurturer on women. Women learn to place the needs of others before their own. If they felt that their abuser was expressing his own emotional pain, they stayed to 'help' their partner and denied their own physical danger.

In addition, Ferraro and Johnson described these six categories as techniques used by women who, like most people in intimate partnerships, work to 'develop through the efforts of each partner to maintain feelings of love and intimacy' (Ferraro and Johnson, 1983: 327). Thus a battered woman's attempts to stay, and the psychological traits she acquired in attempting to stay, were a reflection not of a malformed psychology but, instead, of normality. Changes in circumstances, either in the relationship or in the resources available, spurred women to actively re-evaluate their positions. They point out that this required an enormous amount of effort on the part of the women which was far from the passive stereotype created in earlier research.

Finally, recent work by American therapist Ginny NiCarthy (1987) addressed the psychological factors involved in leaving, including the extent to which women created their own mechanisms for overcoming some of the debilitating emotions and obstacles which prevented their leaving. Moreover, NiCarthy constructs an image of women as survivors, rather than victims. Women who left their abusers had not only 'survived' the abuse but also 'survived' the aftermath of abuse which included depression, anxiety and resurgence of romantic feelings for their partners, as they made the transition into a new lifestyle. Little has been written about how women cope with these struggles, but NiCarthy suggests that the most successful women have formulated complex and skilled methods of psychologically coping. Their 'survival' is an active, progressive effort.[6]

The transition towards viewing battered women as survivors informs the analysis forwarded in Chapter 7 regarding how women transform their past experiences into a positive opportunity for personal growth. This book builds on the concept of 'survivors' and explores the dimensions in which 'survival' can be used to describe the experiences of formerly abused women and those in relationships with abusers.

The development of this psychological analysis reflected, and was reflected in, analyses in other areas of research including that addressed in the following section: sociological perspectives.

Traditional Sociological Research: a Tale of 'Family Violence'

Sociological research over the last 25 years focuses on the social environment which gave rise to woman battering. Conventional sociological theory can be identified by its assumption that the nuclear family unit is a functional social structure created to meet human social needs. This contrasts with feminist sociology, as I will discuss in the next chapter. Sociological studies which gained predominance in the 1970s focused on the social environment of the family unit or community. For the purposes of this book, they are divided into the categories of traditional and feminist; the latter forms the foundation for my study.

The following review shows that the context which is considered worthy of examination differs amongst conventional sociological researchers. The *Newsweek* article is more reflective of psychological approaches than of sociological ones. This suggests that accounts offered to the public not only present mixed and conflated representations of abuse but also may emphasize a particular approach over another. As we will see in the next chapter, such emphasis may be biased to the extent that it excludes an entire area of research.

Throughout the *Newsweek* article there is a running use of terms to denote what happened between Nussbaum and Steinberg which are treated as interchangeable. They range from 'violent relationships' to 'abuse' to 'battering' to 'family violence'. For example, the report of Nussbaum's testimony that her lover's battering had caused the death of their child was entitled 'A Tale of Abuse: Hedda Nussbaum's chilling account of physical and psychological brutality opens disturbing questions about the nature of violent relationships'. Even within this first statement there are a number of different perspectives which are confusingly enmeshed. Although details of the physical and psychological injuries Nussbaum suffered are discussed, it is stated that it was the relationship, rather than Joel Steinberg, that was violent. Moreover, information about child abuse is inset with statistics entitled 'Facts about Family Violence' which include figures about woman abuse and child abuse. These terms, 'violent relationships' and 'family violence', are consistently used to replace more explicit terms, such as 'woman abuse' or 'child abuse', which denote who is being abused and draw attention to who is enacting the abuse.

The words used interchangeably by *Newsweek* are not simply labels for what happened between Steinberg and Nussbaum; they represent specific lines of inquiry and perspective on woman abuse.

American academic interest developed primarily in the field of sociology, rather than psychology as in Britain, and took root in the extension of well established general theories about violence in society to the issue of battering. However, these general theories did not supply detail of the dynamics of battering sufficient to meet the needs of growing public concern. In the mid 1970s sociologists began to assess battering behaviour and relationship dynamics. This led to sociological theories which focused specifically on explaining battering and, as discussed below, placed emphasis on the role of family dynamics in battering rather than the larger social circumstances described by more general theories. Finally, with the introduction of feminist perspectives on the oppression of women, conventional sociological focus in the late 1970s and 1980s incorporated an understanding of how larger structures differently affect each gender. For example, new research focused attention on the extent to which battering is a unidirectional act of violence committed by men against women. This development of thought underlies the conflict we can see in the *Newsweek* report between general terms such as 'family violence', in which the agency of the abuser is not present, and those which more clearly denote who is being abused and who, by implication, is violent, such as 'wife' or 'woman abuse'. Why this specification is important will become evident as we look more closely at the research and its findings.

Sociologists' First Look at Woman Abuse: a Case of Social Violence

One of the first sociological theories about battered women drew on a general sociological model of violence: resource theory. Resource theory attempted to explain all types of violence by suggesting that it was used as a resource when all other sources of power and control were unavailable. Thus violence would have been expected to occur more commonly among the working classes whose economic resources were limited. This model was based on the high incidence of observed and reported violence among the working class. Similarly, a model describing a subculture of violence existing in the working class, in which children learned to be violent (Brown, 1974), was premised on statistics of working class violence. However, such evidence was later to be challenged by studies revealing a high incidence of family violence across all classes (Steinmetz and Straus, 1974).

John O'Brien (1974) argued from his study of 'divorce prone families and violence' that male violence was a result of 'a condition in a family where the achievement ability of the husband [was] less than his proscribed superior status' (p. 71). Thus the male attempted to establish his social status by exerting his dominance over his wife. Much like later feminist analysis that violence against women, including wife beating, is a tool used in the social control and subordination of women by men (Hanmer, 1978; Hanmer and Maynard, 1987), O'Brien based his analysis of battering on the existence of a cultural norm of male dominance. However, he depicted the man as the victim of this cultural norm and suggested that there is a need for 'social intervention of a type intended to strengthen the earning and achievement potential of husbands' (p. 73). Thus, early theories of violence as a form of frustration and assertion were seen to encompass the specific problem of wife abuse, but did not bring under criticism the social circumstances, identified later by feminists, in which violence was used as a tool of domination.

From Society to the Family: 'Facts about Family Violence'
A change in the focus of sociological research involved shifting from incorporating the phenomenon of wife abuse into general models of violence to a focus on the family. With the social concern about child abuse that emerged in the early 1970s, as well as the growth of a shelter movement, sociologists began to investigate how dynamics within the family unit contributed to the use of violence. In America, sociological exploration of child abuse offered a framework in which battering could be studied, independently from the general theories within which the problem had previously been analysed. Thus, in the mid 1970s American research into battering centred on battering as a form of 'family violence' or 'domestic violence'. It is from this branch of research that the terms 'family violence', 'violent relationships' and 'domestic violence' were born.

The first major sociological attempt at quantitative research into battering supported the idea that it was a phenomenon of family dynamics. Within this 1974 study, Richard Gelles rescarched the incidence of, reactions to and dynamics of family violence. Gelles collected his sample of 'violent families' from police and social agency records. Gelles also provided a comparative sample of neighbouring families with no known history of violence.

He recorded a detailed profile of battering within society. He found that violence in the family was more common than previously suspected, as his control group revealed that one-third had experienced violence in some form within the family, and that for one-tenth violence was a regular experience. In accordance with 'resource theory', Gelles found that violence was more prevalent in low income families. However, he ascribed this correlation to an increased amount of stress accompanying low income status, rather than a lack of resources or a subculture of violence. He did not address the fact that violence within low income families may be more likely to come to the attention of police or social services as these families often live in crowded conditions where their violence cannot be kept private. He also failed to examine the possibility that the families he studied were more likely to come into contact with social services, as a result of housing or financial problems, than families in higher income brackets.

Despite these problems, Gelles did provide information about the personal dynamics of battering. Although he used gender neutral terms, such as 'conjugal violence' and 'spouse abuse', Gelles did not ignore the difference between violence perpetrated by men and by women. He concluded that, within violent families, the husband was usually more violent than the wife and that most of the violence by wives was a 'protective reaction' type of violence.[7] He also quantified and categorized the types of violence used, including the use of weapons and threats. He reported the common temporal and spatial locations of such violence and concluded that the isolation of the nuclear family into single family homes allowed for violence to occur in secrecy.

Gelles's results not only provided one of the first detailed and quantified accounts of battering relationships, but also revealed the gender factor in the perpetration of violence that was often ignored in later sociological research of the 1970s. Although Gelles acknowledged the difference between male violence and female self-defence, he constructed a theory of family violence which obscured this. He proposed that social conditioning, experience with violence in one's childhood family and stress from family structure and social position, all contributed to the development of a 'violent family'. Such gender neutral theories led to misconceptions in both the fields of sociology and psychology about why battering occurred, and whether it was the battered women or their partners whose psychology was most significant to the development of a relationship in which a woman was abused.

Later research, of the late 1970s and the 1980s, influenced by feminist analyses, focused on the role of male dominance within Western culture in the use of marital violence to control women, and thus challenged Gelles's model (Breines and Gordon, 1983; Hanmer, 1978; Kalmusst and Straus, 1982).

The focus on family dynamics was adopted by many researchers during the time Gelles formulated and published his work. Thus the issue of domestic violence, as its prevalence was revealed, became acknowledged as a widespread social problem, challenging previous theories which defined battering as deviant behaviour. For instance, sociological researcher Murray Straus, in his foreword to a book by Gelles (1974), recognized that psychological perspectives of wife abuse as deviance did not correspond with the prevalence of the problem. More importantly, Straus argued that models of deviance served to protect the image of the family as a non-violent, peaceful unit of Western culture and thus obscured the high incidence of all forms of family violence, such as wife beating, child abuse and incest. Thus, by the mid 1970s, American research on woman battering was conducted within the fairly narrow focus of family dynamics.

Collaboration between American researchers Gelles, Straus and Steinmetz dominated American sociological research on battered women in the mid 1970s. Sharing the approach of investigating the family as a unit of study, they described the family as a site of conflict and violence rather than one of peace, love and emotional security (Straus, Gelles and Steinmetz, 1980). One way in which these researchers removed the issue of family violence from general studies in violence was to challenge the interaction between economic class and spouse abuse. Steinmetz and Straus (1974), for example, reviewed data suggesting a high level of acceptance of violence in all social classes (also see Stark and McEvoy, 1970). Athough increased frustration might have contributed to violence within the working class, they asserted that attributing causality entirely to social class was 'an example of group stereotyping by social classes' (Steinmetz and Straus, 1974: 10). This 'conflict theory' (Straus, 1980) of family dynamics validated the use of the family as a unit of study, rather than the previous focus on violence as a general social problem or as a characteristic of deviant relationships.

Their 'conflict theory' and the conclusions they draw about 'family violence', however, have not gone unchallenged. The tools used to produce these findings, most notably the conflict tactics scale, have been critiqued in detail by Dobash and Dobash. They point out that the intention of the scale is to measure physical violence, which is defined as 'an act carried out with the intenion, or perceived intention, of causing physical pain or injury to another person' (Dobash and Dobash, 1992: 277). However, the scale focuses exclusively on behaviour and has no capacity by which it might measure intent or perceived intent. This has led to specious conclusions about 'mutual' violence. By looking solely at the acts of hitting, slapping, throwing objects etc., no clue is given as to whether this action is taken or perceived to be as self-defence, as a jest, or with harmful intent. Dobash and Dobash have raised questions about naming men whose wives retaliate after years of abuse 'battered men', as the conflict tactics scale seems to suggest. Lack of contextual information about the physical acts in the results produced by this research tool confounds understanding of wife abuse, according to Dobash and Dobash (1992).

Battering as a Family Phenomenon: the Cycle of Violence
Within the framework of investigating 'family violence', the problems of child abuse and woman abuse were addressed as a single issue and led to hypotheses about how family dynamics were central to both, the legacy of which is evident in the terminology used by *Newsweek*. In addition, this unified approach to child and woman abuse led to theories which proposed a causal relationship between the two. One of the most dominant sociological theories of the mid 1970s into the 1980s was the idea of an intergenerational 'cycle of violence'.

Studies by Straus and Steinmetz showed a high correlation between childhood experience with domestic violence and later experience with violence in adult relationships. They called this transmittal of violence the 'cycle of violence' and proposed that exposure to violence within the family predisposes children to create a violent relationship in adulthood. Steinmetz (1977a), for example, concluded from her research that children learned to resolve conflicts in a manner similar to that exhibited by their parents in interactions and disciplining methods.

A major flaw in her work on 'the cycle of violence' arises from the fact that it was based on gender neutral investigations which confounded the difference between learning to be a batterer and learning to be battered.[8] As a result, some subsequent investigations into the learning of family violence focused specifically on the effect of marital violence on one sex and reported that men learned to be aggressors whereas women learned to be victims. From this perspective, the 'cycle' theory was similar to psychological theories which suggested that women 'chose' a violent relationship. Indeed this perspective evidently still persists and has been expanded to include any woman who has had an unstable or frightening childhood. *Newsweek* suggests a connection between Nussbaum's childhood fear of abandonment and the possibility that she 'may have been particularly susceptible to the influence of a domineering man' (p. 60). The study of whether children from violent homes were predisposed to enter violent relationships with abusive partners was a primary issue reflected in research throughout the 1970s and 1980s. But the data provided were far from conclusive.

For example, Gelles reported that women who experienced violence in their families as children were more likely to become victims of abuse (Gelles 1979). However, the quantitative evidence from which he drew this correlation was not conclusive. Of the 54 women who experienced no violence in childhood, 46 per cent became victims, and of the 12 women who reported violence in childhood, 66 per cent became victims. Neither the size of the population Gelles studied, nor the difference between the incidence of victimization between the two, suggests that the correlation was particularly strong. Gelles's 1976 study, in fact, indicated that experience with family violence in childhood, rather than rendering a woman more vulnerable to entering an abusive relationship, instead was the most reliable predictive factor (among the five factors he studied) of whether a wife seeks intervention, divorce or separation from the violent relationship.

In response to studies which show a stronger correlation between childhood abuse and victimization as an adult (Walker, 1984; Beck et al., 1982; Prescott and Letko, 1977), Pagelow (1981a) argued that such findings provided specious information because they did not address the difference between observing violence as a child and being a victim of parental violence. She reported that there was no correlation between observing battering and entering a battering relationship later in life. Furthermore, she asserted that there may have been a negative correlation between being a victim of family violence as a child and staying in a violent conjugal relationship. In other words, victims of child abuse were more likely to leave their batterer sooner than women who were not abused as children. Although evidence of the effect of childhood violence on the behaviour of adult men was more con-clusively in support of the 'cycle' theory, women's learning of the victim role was questionable.

In general, American sociological focus on the family ignored the larger social constructs which supported male battering of women. Contemporary British research was primarily dichotomized by the psychological studies produced by writers such as Gayford and Pizzey and the feminist analyses which were developed from refuge work and feminist theories about women's oppression.

Notes

1 As with some of the work noted in sociological research, this chapter notably within my discussion of 'survivors', overlaps with literature reflecting feminist approaches. Clearly some of the work in each of the two sections of this chapter is influenced by feminist ideas. However, I distinguish between these and the literature reviewed in the first section of Chapter 2 by reserving work which expresses an explicit feminist approach and draws heavily from feminist scholarship for my review of 'feminist approaches'.

2 *Newsweek* had, for example, a circulation of 3,224,770 in the US and 34,000 in the British Isles in 1991, according to the Audit Bureau of Circulations.

3 In particular, *Time* magazine, December 1988, presented the issues, but a review of *New Statesman*, *Society* and *The Economist* yielded no major articles on this trial.

4 This is not the first period in which wife abuse was the focus of a social movement and public concern. In the mid to late 1800s US and British feminists argued for divorce rights to be granted to women and they supported this argument largely by citing the violence women suffered at the hands of their husbands (Dobash and Dobash, 1980; Mazzola, 1987; Sutton, 1979). Moreover, John Stuart Mill and Francis Power Cobbe fuelled a public debate about the status of women in marriage which rendered them vulnerable to violence (Dobash and Dobash, 1980; Mazzola, 1987). It is important to recognize that the information presented here reflects the present day social context in which it was gathered and is only one part of a history of women's experiences of and struggles to be free from abuse.

5 'Learned helplessness' is a psychological term that, before Walker's work, referred specifically to the reaction of dogs who were electrically shocked while in a cage with no escape. These dogs responded to repeated trials by learning to be passive. Finally, even when a method of escape was made available, they no longer made an attempt to free themselves from the shocks. It was concluded that they 'learnt to be helpless'. Breines and Gordon (1983) criticized Walker for generalizing the laboratory behaviour of dogs to the behaviour of battered women. They pointed out that laboratory behaviour of a

non-human species could not be taken as representative of human behaviour in a situation which is socially, emotionally and structurally complex, such as woman battering.

6 Studies which revealed the ways in which women took control over their lives, and thus could have been more accurately described as 'survivors' than as 'victims', added an important perspective to psychological understanding of the experience and behaviour of battered women. However, such studies may also have contributed to a new mode of narrow-mindedness that had characterized previous theories of 'masochism' and 'victimism'. Barry explains: 'To recognize women as survivors is not enough. There is a difference between survival and effective survival. Effective survival necessitates women's coming together over the serious threat of . . . violence and organizing against it' (1979: 42). In other words, exclusive focus on the psychological efforts of individual women which allowed them to survive their circumstances may have obscured the need to investigate and change the social circumstances which supported battering.

7 For example, women may attack their partners or use a weapon with the intent to disable them in order to reduce or prevent violence that they predict will be inflicted in future. Furthermore, Gelles reported that violence by husbands is more likely to be one-way and is perpetrated regardless of whether a woman fights back or not.

8 This gender neutrality produced confusion which can be found in the work of professionals who, within the provision of service to battered women, forwarded theories about husband battering (Cantoni, 1981).

2
Towards a New Perspective

Feminist Approaches to Understanding Woman Abuse

Missing from the perspectives and terminology used in the *Newsweek* feature to discuss woman abuse is the vast literature on feminist theory and practice. I have noted where feminist psychological and socio- logical approaches have had an impact on the conventional research in these fields and where this impact is evident in the news report. However, these are part of a larger body of thought based on theory and practical experience in the social movement for abused women.

Although feminist thought consists of many disciplines and per- spectives, a distinct body of analysis concerning woman battering can be identified as feminist. Specifically, feminist analysis has, as its central core, the premise that woman battering is an expression and a mechanism of the institutional oppression of women. According to this approach, women are systematically and structurally controlled by men within a culture that is designed to meet the needs of and benefit men. Thus, the meaning of male violence against women, including woman battering, cannot be addressed through the perspectives of individual victimization or relationship dynamics. The extent and rigidity of the social structure which underlies battering has been identified through two main approaches: that which focuses on women's position within the family, and that which investigates violence against women in general.

In the previous chapter, we have seen similar strands of thought: general theories of violence applied to battering, and analyses of violence in the family which are applied to battering. Functionalism, for example, is fundamental to many of the analyses presented previously; it is the perspective that the structures observed in society serve essential functions, be it biological, psychological, individual or social functions. Parsons describes the nuclear family as being one structure which was created to serve these essential functions (Durkheim, 1984; Spencer, 1987). However, Parsons's theories and functionalism in general have been criticized by feminists. In particu- lar, such theorists assume that the structures observed in society are functional. Feminists argue that, rather than existing because it serves an essential function, the nuclear family may be maintained and enforced by a system of patriarchy which serves to grant men greater power over and in relation to women.[1] One main issue of this debate, for instance, was Parsons's assertions that the sexual division of labour existing in the 1950s was functional to society because it helped maintain the structure of the nuclear family. Feminists argue that such a division was not inherently functional; rather it served the purpose of keeping women economically dependent on men and in a lower position of economic power than men. In this way it did, in fact, secure the existence of the family. But the nuclear family, rather than serving a primary function of tension management, as argued by Parsons, was seen by feminists to be part of a patriarchal system (Friedan, 1963; Johnson, 1989; Delphy and Leonard, 1992).

Delphy and Leonard have developed this argument further to demonstrate how the family is part of the exploitative system of labour relations. They argue that unpaid housework is often incorrectly compared directly to paid work and, if acknowledged at all, is placed within the context of the public economic system. Yet, they point out that this comparison ignores the relations of power within the family in which women are often dependent upon and abused by their partners. Women are also vulnerable within this system because, in contrast to the case in employment, one does not normally seek a new family if working conditions are unfavourable. These 'bad things' about women's labour often 'get lost' in analysing women's unpaid labour within traditional economic theory. The authors show how the economic system of the family differs from the public system in terms of what is exchanged and how these exchanges are negotiated, and how this system supports women's subordination (Delphy and Leonard, 1992).

Functionalism underlies much of the work of Gelles, Straus and Steinmetz presented in the previous chapter. They probe for answers to the question 'Why have families in which abuse occurs ceased to be functional?' or 'What are the social pressures that have served to distort what is otherwise an inherently functional social structure?' It is this underlying functionalist view which feminists contest in their analysis not only of woman abuse, but also of the family as a site of women's oppression.

Feminist theory differs from traditional sociological inquiry because it takes as central a critical analysis of the system of male domination, and how it relates to woman abuse.[2] Clearly, not all feminists hold to one perspective on woman abuse (see *Ms*, April 1989, for example). What I present here represents two major strands of work which are held as central to the analysis of women's oppression. In addition, I will explore how these approaches have been challenged and how information from refuges and shelters shows the need for broadening feminist approaches to understanding woman abuse. In the second section of this chapter I will look at the importance of research methods to feminist analyses of abuse.

Theoretical Frameworks Applied to Wife Battering

The body of thought outlined below addresses the ways in which women are oppressed and how men benefit from abuse of women in intimate relationships. Primarily, theories draw upon the social elements or circumstances which contribute to or develop from the existence of woman battering, in order to show how woman abuse is part of women's subordination. Of the many feminist perspectives on battering that have arisen, I will focus on two of the most prominent: on battering as a part of women's oppression within the family, and on woman battering as a specific example of male violence against women.

Feminist Analysis of the Family and Battering   Many feminists have critiqued both the ideology and the structure of the 'traditional', one-income, two-parent, heterosexual family (Barrett and McIntosh, 1982; Branca, 1975; Gittins, 1985; Hooks, 1984; Segal, 1983). Not only is the 'traditional' ideology unrepresentative of the experience of many women, but society is organized such that women who do not conform to this structure are denied acknowledgement within social institutions. Gittins illustrates this perspective:

> legislation has developed in such a way that it has become more difficult for individuals to live alone or with members of the same sex. Social disapproval, financial discrimination and fear of interference by social workers and police in non-heterosexual households – particularly those where children are involved – put very strong pressures on both men and women – but especially women – to live in some sort of family. (1985: 153)

A major component of the feminist critique of the institution of marriage and the two-parent heterosexual family has been to show the ways in which this ideology supports and enforces a family structure in which women are oppressed. One of the most graphic illustrations of such oppression in the family is woman battering. Thus, in this approach, battering is seen as a problem which has developed out of social ideology and structures which enforce the 'traditional' family.

R.E. and R.P. Dobash were the first to base an analysis on the idea of male domination in their book *Violence against Wives: a Case against the Patriarchy* (1980). It is within this study that Dobash and Dobash focused on what 'traditional ideas' are about and how such ideas support an institution of patriarchy in which wife abuse is a major form of control over women by men. They also argued that 'the family', and women's positions as wives, are part of this institution.

Within the field of sociology, Dobash and Dobash challenged the traditional methodologies which gave rise to theories of 'family violence'. Much of the data they collected were similar to those obtained by past researchers, e.g. categorization and quantification of types of resulting injuries. However, they asserted 'it is in the marital setting that women are most likely to become involved in violence, and this is usually as victims and not attackers. It is in the institution of the family that patriarchal legacy persists through continuation of the hierarchical relationship between men and women' (Dobash and Dobash, 1978: 432).

They argued that the historical legacy of men's legal ownership of their wives, along with the laws which specifically gave men the right to abuse or 'punish' them, underlay the social circumstances in which wives were the 'appropriate' victims of battering. Evidence for this analysis included the finding that abuse began, in many cases, only after the couple had been married (Dobash and Dobash, 1980). Since this finding, others have found that police and court records showed that some abusers believed they had a legal and moral right to be brutal towards the women to whom they were married (Ptacek, 1988).[3]

From interviewing 137 battered wives, Dobash and Dobash cited a number of findings which indicated that battering is a way in which men control women and is part of a larger system of control. For example, they showed that increased social isolation was a characteristic of a battering relationship applied only to the woman. Men were more likely to increase the frequency with which they socialized with their own friends, whereas women decreased contact with friends over the period of the relationship. Furthermore, Dobash and Dobash documented how women were not passive, or 'helpless', in the relationship. They sought many forms of aid in reducing the danger of their situation, although the type of aid they requested or received was restricted. Women reported that they were less likely to contact agencies such as social workers and police because of the stigma attached to the use of such agencies in domestic matters. They also reported that many of the agencies contacted responded with concern about keeping the family together, held stereotypes about the masochistic psychology of battered women, and treated the effects of abuse rather than attempting to secure a safer situation for the women. Other researchers have explored in more detail the response of helping agencies to battered women and have confirmed many of the results reported in *Violence against Wives* (Hanmer, 1988; Johnson, 1985; Prescott and Letko, 1977; Roy, 1977). Thus Dobash and Dobash asserted that battering was a product of a system which was reflected in historical laws about male ownership and marriage, as well as current social gender roles and structures which secured the dominance of men over women.[4] Given that abuse occurs within, is a product of and helps reinforce this patriarchal social context, that it is described as 'woman abuse' or 'wife abuse' rather than 'family violence' is extremely significant. The former reveal the direction of violence and, as a result, highlight the position of women within the relationships, echoing the historical and social oppression of women in general. By contrast the current use of the latter, in obscuring this connection, serves to silence the link between women's oppression and their experiences of abuse in relationships which is so well documented in the Dobash and Dobash study.

But some more recent studies reflect an implicit acknowledgement in that they have addressed aspects of the role of women's oppression in the dynamics and social circumstances surrounding battering.[5] Three types of study are particularly illustrative of the ways in which insight into cultural systems of oppression affected general sociological research: those which addressed women's social dependency on men, as prescribed by cultural roles, and its place in battering (Homer et al., 1985; Kalmusst and Straus, 1982); those which explored the inter-action of social status in husband and wife relations that 'predisposed' a couple to stress and violence (Hornung et al., 1981; Ylló, 1984); and those which focused on ways in which battered women sought help in escaping the violence, and the inappropriate reactions by social agencies which served to reinforce women's entrapment in a violent relationship (Homer et al., 1985; Pahl, 1978; Prescott and Letko, 1977). Such studies are not explicitly focused on a theory of women's subordination and the ways in which men benefit from women's oppression within this system. But they are informed by feminist theory in their analysis of the way in which battering is a phenomenon created and maintained, in part, by the larger social structure.

The interchangeable use of terms illustrated by *Newsweek* is, in fact, a conflation of very distinct research approaches. At present the two major contending perspectives are the 'family violence' approach (Gelles and Straus, 1988) and the 'woman abuse' or 'wife abuse' approach. Clearly there is debate over which conceptualization is most appropriate for investigating abuse of women: the family unit or women's oppression. The concurrent use of terminology from both approaches in the media presents a confusing, contradictory des-cription of abuse to the public.

The phrase 'wife abuse' has been used with reservations recently in feminist work on the family or male violence (Bograd, 1988; Dobash and Dobash, 1988; Edwards, 1987; Saunders, 1988; Ylló, 1988). Questions have arisen as to how useful this phrase is in describing women who are neither wives, nor planning to become wives, nor cohabiting with their abusers, or who are in lesbian relationships, and who experience severe and repeated attacks within intimate relation-ships (Lobel, 1986; McShane, 1988; NiCarthy, 1987; Pagelow, 1981a).[6]

Like married women, these women are denied the opportunity to express their need for help, because they are silenced by their own shame and because little aid is offered through either formal or informal channels.

Unquestioned, exclusive focus on abused women as wives may, in fact, contribute to the silencing of women's experiences.

> Some of the names that have been applied to domestic violence caused problems for some women. Wife beating implies that violence only happens to married women . . . In some situations, women . . . felt abused but were unable to name their experience at the time. (Kelly, 1988a: 120)

So, a cultural ideology based upon hierarchical family structures may be one relevant factor in the social construction of woman abuse. Certainly both marital and non-marital relationships are centred around an ideology of sexual hierarchy which is symbolized by the cultural images of the marital relationship. Furthermore, the cultural values underlying marriage and corresponding legislation provide a common context in which both marital and non-marital relationship structures are formed.[7] As such, insight into the ways in which this contributes to woman battering is important, although it is becoming apparent that it is not sufficient as a sole focus of developing feminist understanding.

Feminist Analysis of Battering as a Specific Example of 'Violence against Women'   A second major approach of feminist analysis on battering is the application of a general theory on male violence against women to the specific example of battering. This approach reveals how violence is enacted on any woman, rather than just wives, and thus provides an important supplement to the analyses based on the history and structure of the family. The connection between different forms of violence against women distinguishes woman abuse from other forms of violence, child abuse or violence between men. Because violence against women occurs within a specific cultural context and contributes to women's status relative to men, it has a specific meaning.

In America, the anti-rape movement originated in the early 1970s and preceded the movement for battered women. Contemporary with sociological analysis of violence as a 'family dynamic', feminists in America were developing a wider approach to understanding male violence against women. Major works on the politics of rape, such as Susan Brownmiller's *Against Our Will* (1975) and Griffin's 'Rape: the all American crime' (1971), showed that women were defined through their sexuality and that it was this sexuality that men strove aggressively to control and dominate. The politics of rape were compared to that of terrorism (Griffin, 1971), in which all individuals of the group targeted for attack were kept under control by the threat of violence (Edwards, 1987). This analysis had been extended to other forms of violence such that control was said to be expressed through 'institutionalized violence' (Richardson and Taylor, 1983) or a continuum of violence (Kelly, 1988b), which included pornography (Dworkin, 1981), rape, sexual harassment and battering. Some feminists have extended this analysis to an examination of the social construction of heterosexuality by arguing that the compulsory nature of heterosexuality in a homophobic culture underpins the opportunity for male control over women in intimate relationships as well as within the culture at large (Dworkin, 1987; Griffin, 1981; Pharr, 1988). The creation of a term which included all types of violence against women was integral to communicating that such violence was linked to serve a common social purpose: the maintenance of control and domination of women by men.[8] This type of approach to understanding violence against women became popular within both British and American feminist movements (Edwards, 1987; Hanmer, 1978).

Although battering certainly fits within this analysis there are specific aspects of it which stand out as distinct. In the context of a general feminist analysis on institutionalized violence, focus is often placed on the ways in which violence serves as a threat to all women. For example, because of the threat of rape, most women feel they must confine their movements to locations and circumstances in which rape seems less likely to occur. Thus, women do not go out alone at night, or they are fearful and vigilant if they do (Hanmer and Saunders, 1984). But abuse of women by their partners does not seem to hold the same threat to women in general as do other forms of violence against women. Women do not seem to approach marriage and relationships with the same hypervigilance and sense of vulnerability as they do in entering the public realm.

In Britain, where the analysis of violence against women developed from a framework of feminist thought about child and woman abuse rather than an extension of perspectives on rape, the complexity of the status of woman abuse is addressed. Hanmer and Saunders (1986) describe how the beliefs held by women, and constructed socially, about violence and danger to women in the public arena encourage women to seek protection from men, 'the very group that abuses them' (Hanmer and Saunders, 1986: 29), and urge them to escape to the private arena, their homes, where in fact they are more vulnerable to violence. They assert that these paradoxes underlie how 'male violence against women is socially constructed to perpetuate itself' (Hanmer and Saunders, 1986: 29). Woman abuse then has a complex role within the system through which institutionalized violence against women is maintained.

Developing Work on Woman Abuse: the Implications of Diversity

Feminists have begun to address the problems involved in using the term 'wife abuse', particularly those working in refuges or services which aid a diversity of women. Many specific groups of women have challenged the generalizability of the theories discussed above and have aided the development of feminist analysis. Services for refugee women, for example, have begun to expose how the threat of deportation can play a role in the exertion of power by abusive partners (NWIRP, 1992). Advocates for deaf women have revealed that many deaf women are forced to stay silent about their abuse for fear of rejection from the community or retaliation by their partners who are more likely to discover their disclosure because of the high degree of interconnectedness within the deaf community (ADWAS, 1992). In the US many Native American women face the shame of speaking out about abuse to their communities, in which, before the interference of white culture, woman battering was extremely rare. Despite action for change, many Native American women still may be unable to utilize protective or support services, either because they are isolated geographically, if they live on certain reservations, or because lack of cultural sensitivity in available services renders them inaccessible (Allen, 1986). The nature of control exerted over women through abuse is multi-dimensional and often incorporates the use of power gained through circumstances set up by more than one type of oppression. Below I will discuss in greater detail two areas in which feminist theory has begun to address this complexity.

Recent work has documented the isolation, brutality, undirectionality of violence and aspects of control characterizing woman abuse which occur within lesbian relationships (Lobel, 1986; NiCarthy, 1987). Barbara Hart suggests that the power dynamics fundamental to heterosexual relationships in a patriarchal society, which lay the foundation for abuse, also influence the dynamic of lesbian relationships exposed to that patriarchal structure:

> Lesbians, like non-lesbians, often desire the control over the resources and decisions in family life that power brings and that violence can assure when control is resisted. The same elements of hierarchy of power, ownership, entitlement and control exist in lesbian family relationships. Largely this is true because lesbians have also learned that violence works in achieving partner compliance. (Hart in Lobel, 1986: 175)

This analysis suggests that relationships between women that occur within a patriarchal social structure can result in one partner using the tools of power, such as domestic violence, traditionally used by men to control women. Furthermore, the same gender roles and economic structures that keep battered women in abusive relationships with men also may be experienced by lesbians such that leaving their partner is difficult.[9]

Introduction of the topic of violence in lesbian relationships is a potentially volatile issue because it illustrates that women can be controlled by violence and abuse by other women, rather than solely by those benefiting from their dominant position in society: men. When it was first introduced, many feminists felt the issue of lesbian battering weakened the powerful work of radical feminists on the oppression of women through compulsory heterosexuality (Dworkin, 1987) and, more generally, analyses of the connection between male domination and male violence. Furthermore, admission of violence between women was avoided as it was felt such information could potentially provide fuel for homophobic attitudes. Thus one challenge to feminist theory, which has just begun to be acknowledged, is how to adjust the analysis in order to fully address the issue of violence perpetrated by women against their female partners.

A second challenge has been raised by women oppressed by racism. I will address specifically the concerns raised by Afro-American and Afro-Caribbean women as an example of the ways in which racism can introduce new issues into theorizing about abuse because of the wealth of material available on Afro-American perspectives. The specific nature of their struggles is not assumed to depict the many ways in which racism impacts woman abuse. One dilemma faced by African American women is in identifying with feminists who speak of men as the oppressors. The Combahee River Collective (1982) explains:

> Our situation as black people necessitates that we have solidarity around the fact of race, which white women of course do not need to have with white men, unless it is their negative solidarity as racial oppressors. We struggle together with black men against racism, while we also struggle with black men about sexism. (p.14)

Other African American feminists describe similar feelings about being torn between working with white women and working with black men (Hooks, 1984; Hull et al., 1982).[10] This tension produces an atmosphere in which black feminists and black battered women feel restricted in describing their experience of being both racially and sexually oppressed.

Moreover, because violence within partnerships is seen by many black people to stem from the stress experienced by black men in a white racist culture, African American women may experience a pressure from their communities to understand and forgive their partners. Hooks, for example, describes a cycle in which African

American men express their frustration about oppression in the workplace by enacting violence towards their partners. These abused women, then, may be accepting of the violence as part of their commitment to the common struggle against racism (Hooks, 1984). This perspective is highly debated amongst African American feminists. Evelyn C. White (1985; 1986), for instance, calls for a recognition of how this ethic, along with racist stereotypes of black women, weakens rather than strengthens their communities. In doing so, she asserts that the issue of racism is central to the experiences of African American battered women in that they must begin to question how the expectation of 'strong black womanhood' (White, 1986: 12), which encourages women to bear abuse in the name of black struggle, is itself exploitative. Another issue of particular relevance to black women is that the options available to them in protecting themselves are limited as a result of the racist culture in which they live. Amina Mama documents how, in London, black women hesitate to call on police for protection because of the possible racist attacks by police on themselves and their partners and because of the reluctance of police to enforce the law on behalf of Afro-Caribbean people (Mama, 1989b).[11] Thus a feminist analysis of battering requires an exploration not only of how battering may be seen as a tool of oppression used by men, but also of how this translates into the experience of African American and Afro-Caribbean women who are racially as well as sexually oppressed.[12]

The dilemmas facing battered lesbians, African American women and Afro-Caribbean women challenge theories about male violence against women, and criticisms of the conventional family structure, as applied to battering. It is clear that these do not yet adequately address overlapping systems of oppression such as racism and heterosexism.

Feminist Practice and Knowledge about Formerly Abused Women

A significant part of our knowledge about abused women is provided by the information collected by refuges, or researchers working closely with refuges, about the experiences of women after leaving abusers (Binney at al., 1981; Hoff, 1990; NWAF, 1977; Pahl, 1985a; 1985b; Schechter, 1982; WAFE, 1979). It is based on first-hand experience with battered women who have left their abusers, as well as on the contributions of formerly battered women who are involved in the movement. This underpublicized information speaks to the question provocatively asked by *Newsweek* about Nussbaum: 'Why was a battered woman powerless to escape – even when her own children were in danger?' (WAFE, 1979: 56). In addition to psychological explanations, refuge and shelter staff offer detailed information concerning the practical reasons why women find leaving abusive partners extremely difficult.

In general, refuges that aid abused women focus on the needs and issues these women confront within the first months to a year after leaving their partners, as this is the period in which they are in contact with such organizations. This work has practical focus rather than being theory based. It focuses on what the women need and how refuges may best go about meeting these needs or facilitating women's efforts to meet their own needs. It demonstrates that there are an enormous number of issues confronting abused women who have left their abusers which have gone almost entirely unacknowledged by the bulk of current research. The information, as will be described below, hints that once abused women have left their partners, their battles to attain independence, rather than having been won, have just entered a new phase. Thus the question 'Why didn't she leave?', which presumes leaving to be a final solution to the problem, is misdirected and misinformed. The specific nature of women's struggles once they *have* left their partners is the focus of the study. The most detailed work regarding this issue, to date, comes from UK refuges, and includes the work of Jan Pahl and the Women's Aid Federation, England.

In 1985, Pahl's research findings revealed the nature of women's experience of refuge life in England. She found that, although many particularly valued independence and the peacefulness of non-violence, a significant number experienced loneliness, poverty and boredom. The pain associated with these are products of a culture which is based economically and socially on married couples or two-parent families. The women also reported that they thought financial dependence was somewhat inevitable. All women wanted some form of paid work but the expense and lack of child care facilities forced them to rely mainly on social security or low earnings supplemented by their ex-partner's income. Finally, many found refuge information to be appropriate to their needs, including how to apply for housing, what legal rights women were entitled to, and the options available for financial support (Pahl, 1985b).[13]

Moreover, the use of refuge experience in investigating the long-term problems faced by women has been particularly valuable, as women often return to refuges for support and information. Thus refuges are a contact point for the somewhat invisible population of formerly battered women. Their information indicates that formerly abused women may face social isolation, economic deprivation, seemingly endless problems with state service agencies, and difficulties in establishing new intimate relationships as a result of the emotional scars of abuse (Binney et al., 1981; NWAF, 1977). This suggests that leaving and establishing an independent life is not a one-step solution but rather a long-term process which includes defining 'freedom' from violence within the confines of a society that is structured to meet the needs of men, not single women and mothers. It is the aim of the study presented here to explore in detail how this is so and how women cope with these challenges.

Insight gleaned from women's refuges has begun to be supported by research. A recent US study by Hoff (1990) investigated the first year of women's lives after leaving abusers, and the responses to women and values about violence in the family held by support network members: friends, family, refuge staff, counsellors, nurses, social workers, physicians, police and priests. She concluded that often part of the problem faced by formerly abused women was in attaining respectful, empathic and appropriate support from network members. Moreover, she addressed the ways in which policies which enforced women's dependency on men or the state presented obstacles to women upon leaving their abusers. She described formerly abused women who left shelters as 'poor and homeless', accentuating the degree to which practical problems were at the forefront of their lives, and how these were related to a social structure which encouraged women's dependence. Some of the details of her findings will be presented in later chapters.

Upon recontacting the women five years after the study, Hoff revealed that the aftermath of abuse was still a prominant part of their lives. The practical issues of housing and finances, as well as the emotional impact of abuse, were still central issues for formerly abused women. She calls for a study which explores the long-term results of 'wife battering' on women and their children in order to understand how we may act to change the formal and social support of formerly abused women such that their short- and long-term needs are not so acutely denied.

In sum, then, in order to understand the full meaning of woman abuse we need to begin to explore the nature of women's struggle both during *and* once they have ended their relationships with abusers. Nussbaum's story has been offered to the public up to the point in which she became free from her abuser and testified in court against him. There is a cursory mention by *Newsweek* of her recuperation in a hospital in New York. But the nature of this process remains outside the concern of news reports. Yet, according to the experiences of other abused women, Nussbaum's story cannot have ended with the news-breaking headlines of her court trials. A complete portrayal of women's experience of abuse, as well as feminist analysis of woman abuse, require investigation not only of what it means to live in a society which supports abuse and the variety of dilemmas faced by a diversity of women, but also of what it means to free oneself from an abuser within this society. The social context of abuse does not simply affect women who are being abused but also is experienced by women who have acted to free themselves from abuse. Only by exploring this aspect of women's experiences can we begin to fully understand abuse in its larger social context and the degree to which it affects women's lives.

In this book I hope to provide a much fuller picture of the nature of women's experiences of abuse by exploring those of formerly abused women, and looking at the impact on women of abuse and leaving an abuser.

The Basis of Creating a Feminist Approach

Concurrent with the development of the research and theory which I have described as feminist has been that of research methodology which has challenged traditional conventions. In this section I will briefly discuss the relation between feminism and the research methodology and then move on to explain the ways in which my research draws from this.

Feminism and the Research Methodology
The bulk of feminist discussion concerning methodology focuses on the way in which it differs from traditional research methodologies of a variety of disciplines. These critiques have developed out of the premise that the methodologies of traditional disciplines are inappropriate for the study of women's oppression. In general, this is so because traditional sociological methodologies have been developed using a language and with an emphasis on objectivity that precludes fully exploring the experiences of women (Graham, 1986; Harding, 1986, Oakley, 1981; Spender, 1981; Stanley and Wise, 1979). Thus, at present, the idea of a feminist methodology consists of a diverse spectrum of specific techniques, theories and epistemologies which have grown out of this critique and offer alternative ways of researching women (Harding, 1981; Kelly, 1988b; Stanley, 1990).[14]

Feminists have argued that for research to be feminist it must, in some way, contribute to the political movement. This may take the form of a contribution to knowledge about the ways in which women are controlled in a male dominated culture, the ways in which women experience such control, the ways that they cope with it, or simply the nature of women's experience in cultures that place primary importance on the needs and experiences of men. Different researchers hold different definitions of what may be considered a contribution to the struggle against oppression. Many assert that research must also be closely linked with action, such as involving the participants in projects which use the research and actively contribute to change for women (Mies, 1983; Lather, 1988; Stanley, 1990). But underlying all feminist research is the aim to understand, and thus bring forward for examination, the position and experiences of women that are often ignored or misinterpreted in cultures where information is controlled by men.

In meeting this aim, feminist research strives to adopt methods of approach which allow women's experiences to become visible. In relation to the use of interview techniques, an important example of such feminist research techniques is the use of 'story-telling'. Hilary Graham asserts that one of women's typical forms of communication is the telling of stories. Thus the typical interview format of fragmented questions does not allow women to communicate in a familiar way, and tends to inhibit their ability to communicate their experience. In addition, Graham suggests that the information flows between the interviewee and the interviewer set up a power imbalance similar to that present in general society in which men produce and govern the distribution of knowledge (Graham, 1984). Traditional interviewing techniques, then, have the potential to re-create the power imbalance that exists between men and women in society (Finch, 1984; Graham, 1984; Oakley, 1981; Ramazanoglu, 1989; Scott, 1984). In re-creating this imbalance, research which focuses on interviewing women may further the oppression of women by reaffirming their reduced access to power. Thus feminist research strives to adopt new ways of interviewing in which this power hierarchy is not an integral part of the way in which women's experience is explored and expressed (Finch, 1984; Graham, 1984; Oakley, 1981).

Moreover, according to feminist researchers, the use of interview methodologies has a specific relation to the objectives of feminist political action. For example, Stanley and Wise suggest that feminist interviewing methods not only are data-collecting strategies, but also have a relation to the consciousness raising and self-examination central to the feminist movement. They assert that 'accounts of the personal constitute, not only a realm for examination and discussion, but also the subject matter of feminist theory and thus the basis of feminist political activity' (Stanley and Wise, 1979: 360). In this way, feminist research methodologies are deeply rooted in the feminist movement and recognize that interview techniques used in exploring women's experiences are related not only to research but also to the beliefs underlying the feminist movement.

Kelly, in reference to Laws (1986), offered a basic definition of feminist research which speaks to the fundamental beliefs motivating it and the wealth of the critique of traditional methodologies:

Laws asserts that what distinguishes feminist research is the theoretical framework underlying it. She suggests a minimal definition of feminism as 'a belief that women are oppressed and a commitment to end that oppression' . . . For research to be feminist it must be predicated on both the theoretical premise and the practical commitment: its purpose being to understand women's oppression in order to change it. Feminism is, therefore, both a mode of understanding and a call to action. (1988b: 4)

In formulating my approach to understanding the experiences of formerly abused women, I drew on the specific criticisms of traditional interview techniques described above as well as on the heart of feminist research described by Kelly.

The Research

I chose to use unstructured interviews as a specific form of qualitative inquiry because I wanted to access in-depth information about the complexity of and interaction between women's experiences, feelings, beliefs and actions after leaving abusers. This allowed the interviews to take the form of a conversation, to encourage those interviewed to relate their experiences and attitudes more freely than they might in response to rigid questions (Burgess, 1982; 1984; Whyte, 1982). The need for both an interview environment in which women felt at ease speaking of painful and traumatic experiences or feelings, and a structure which would allow an exploration of a largely unresearched area of women's experiences, called for the use of unstructured interviews which allowed, to some extent, women to change or introduce new topics as seemed appropriate (Burgess, 1982; 1984; Glaser and Strauss, 1967; Whyte, 1982).

I placed only two qualifications on the women I sought: that they had, at some time, been abused by a person with whom they shared an intimate relationship, and that this relationship had been over for a year or more at the time of the interview. I hoped to gain a number of advantages from this. By stipulating that the relationship was 'abusive', I hoped to build upon the knowledge gained by shelters and refuges with which I have come in contact. Specifically, many services for 'battered women' have found that women can be severely terrorized and abused without the use of physical violence by their partners.[15] Moreover, I did not want to contribute to the silencing of women described by Liz Kelly by offering a definition of abuse which they felt did not match their experiences (Kelly, 1987).

A second qualification I placed on the women interviewed was that they should have been out of the relationship for a year or more. I felt this was a clearly defined requirement which would allow me to talk to women who were well established in their independence and not so preoccupied with the practical aspects of leaving and staying away from their partner that they had very little time for retrospection and personal exploration.

Ultimately, I managed to contact a fairly diverse group of 30 women. The group was selected with the desire to respect diversity and allow related themes to arise, not with the intent to find a representative population of formerly abused women. This study, then, speaks to the range of experiences encountered by women who leave abusive partners, rather than providing a generalizable account. (See Appendix 2 for a breakdown of group diversity.)

However, the methods through which I contacted women (see Appendix 1) produced a majority which had been in contact with some kind of empowering service agency, such as a shelter or a particularly supportive one-parent family organization, or had the self-confidence to respond to an advertisement requesting research assistance. Thus the interviews represent a particularly empowered and self-knowing group of women, a factor that no doubt had influence on the positive theme presented in Chapter 7.

Previous to and concurrently with the initial stages of contacting women, I was developing an interview format. I wanted to be able to ask women about specific issues which other research had hinted was of relevance, but also to allow enough freedom in the interviews for women to introduce topics which may not have been documented elsewhere.

I reviewed the few data that had been collected from refuges which have maintained contact with their residents (Binney et al., 1981; Homer et al., 1984; Pahl, 1985b; Welsh Women's Aid, 1980; Ginny NiCarthy, 1987; Janine Turner, 1984). From these sources I drew up a list of questions which addressed the types of problems women had faced.

I also chose to interview each woman twice. I found that other researchers suggested that interviews of an hour to an hour and a half were optimal (Dobash and Dobash, 1978). As I wanted to explore many issues at some depth, one interview of this length with each woman would not have provided sufficient time for discussion. Pilot interviews indicated that a large degree of flexibility was necessary in order to keep the interview flowing in a conversational and relaxed manner. Thus, I condensed the questions into a topic guide (see Appendix 3).

By acknowledging the power women held to decline answering questions and by fitting my topics into their story-telling structure, I allowed the power balance to become less skewed than those identified by feminists. In general, I felt this format was extremely useful in establishing a comfortable and safe atmosphere for women to explore their past with me. Furthermore, it was useful not only in illuminating the interconnections between issues faced by women, but also in allowing new topics to arise and be investigated.

One outcome of allowing women to choose the depth of their disclosures about traumatic experiences, however, is that some participants felt greater distress than they might have with a more structured interview. In response to a follow-up survey (see Appendix 4) three women said my approach allowed them to explore their experiences too deeply for their own comfort. This raises the issue of who takes responsibility for the effect of asking women to probe painful and complex experiences and emotions. For example, one woman found that the memories she shared had taken an extreme physical toll, that an illness which occurred at the time of the abusive relationship had recurred. She felt that the interview had released memories which were much more powerful and damaging than she had expected. This experience underlines the effect interviewing can have on survivors of abuse.[16] Both the format of the unstructured interview, in its similarity to counselling techniques (Egan, 1982; Whyte, 1982),[17] as well as the content itself, can be distressing to women interviewed. Janet Finch remarks on the intimacy and trust gained in interviews conducted by women with women. She reflects on whether this trust between women is potentially exploitative and notes that she 'emerged from the interviews with the feeling that my interviewees needed to know how to protect themselves from people like me' (Finch, 1984). Thus, in interviewing women about their experiences of abuse, leaving an abuser and after leaving, I felt I trod a narrow line between using techniques which allowed some women to speak as fully about their emotional experiences as they wished, and unintentionally guiding women to experience painful and uncomfortable feelings which, without skilled support, may have been damaging to their well-being and health.

With respect to the comments and issues that arose out of this interviewing process, it seems there is a need for more discussion about the responsibility of researchers who study issues that are sensitive or traumatic for their interviewees to provide an environment in which the gain of information to the researcher is not far outweighed by the cost to the women exploring experiences of abuse.

A second issue arising from the nature of the topic under research was my own reaction to it. Feminist researchers have identified the importance of addressing the reactions of the researcher to the research. For example, Stanley and Wise (1983a) described the way in which their reactions to receiving obscene phone calls, eventually presented as 'data', was an integral part of analysing the ways in which women were emotionally attacked and manipulated by men making obscene calls. They noted that explaining and analysing their reactions to the process of research revealed that the actual practice of collecting and analysing 'data' on women's oppression was not as 'hygienic' as it seemed. They, like others, pointed out that the divorce of the researcher from the research emerged from a desire to apply the objectivity, neutrality and standardized research techniques valued in natural sciences to research in the social sciences (Keller, 1985; Warren, 1988). However, they suggested that when such techniques are applied without question to the methodology of social research, one loses a wealth of information and insight.

Liz Kelly also identifies the need to address the responses of the researcher to the research process. She identifies this aspect of methodology as 'reflexive experiential analysis':

> Moving between the interviews and my own experiences and reactions was an integral part of the research methodology. Had I 'tuned out' these responses I would probably not have noticed or understood the importance of aspects of women's experience of sexual violence. (1988b: 19)

In conducting the interviews which form the basis of this book, my emotions and attitudes underwent a tremendous change. The act of exploring women's experiences of abuse was tremendously stressful. Although on the one hand I was inspired and moved by the strength and insights demonstrated by the women I spoke with, on the other I became intensely aware of the fact that abuse in a relationship can happen to any woman in a variety of subtle forms. I began to question my own relationships and became aware of the degree to which most intimate relationships are founded on a balance of power that can easily be shifted such that one partner becomes abused. I also felt extremely confused about my own use of power in intimate relationships and began to question at a very deep level the comfortable, dichotomous position I had held previously about men being the abusers and women being the victims. This confusion encouraged me to listen more closely to women's perceptions of the dynamics of abuse in their own lives. Thus I began to uncover the complexities of abuse in relationships which had not been emphasized in the research I had read previously.

I also reviewed my own experience of relationships. Memories continually emerged of relationships which I had thought of as basically loving and healthy but in which I began to remember specific elements that reminded me of the emotional abuse women described. These included jealousy expressed by my partner in one of my first intimate relationships; feeling, as a child, that I had to choose between offering loyalty to either my mother or my father in the context of their disagreements and conflicts; and recognition of deep wells of rage toward loved ones which had been unsafe to express or to feel· in past relationships. Only by disentangling the emotions I felt in response to these memories and recognizing their origins could I begin to apply them to understanding my research. In time, rather than being confused and overwhelmed by my own sense of anger, I could recognize its source and use it to empathize with women's descriptions of rage and desire for revenge. Ultimately, my emotions led me to a fuller understanding of women's subjective reality.

Another aspect of my emotional response which informed my analysis was my heightened sensitivity to films and television programmes. I found that I refused to attend films which focused on violence or abuse. In one sense, I felt this was a tragic loss of access to information about societal attitudes. I battled with myself over opportunities to see films which either focused on attitudes towards violence against women or glamorized the role of abuse in intimate relationships. I grew averse to television programmes, many of which seemed to depict emotional abuse as humorous in ways I had not noticed previously. Any exposure to films which contained such issues, and experience of an audience reaction of enjoyment of scenes of abuse, filled me with a sense of rage about the cultural attitudes with which we live. Such experiences also brought on intense feelings of alienation from society generally.

This heightened sensitivity was virtually impossible to explain to others who had not experienced or explored the issue of abuse, and thus cut me off from any dialogue about my feelings or reactions with others who had watched the same programmes. The experience illuminated the extent to which abuse is integral to cultural notions about relationships as discussed in Chapter 6. It also reflected women's accounts of the isolation that accompanies abuse, because there were no culturally recognized words to communicate my feelings about and reactions to the representations of emotional abuse.

I could not have divorced my own reactions from the research process. Instead, the availability of the experience of other researchers, such as that outlined by Kelly (1988b), and the recognition of the importance of researcher involvement, allowed me to recognize and use my reactions as an invaluable tool of analysis by deepening my awareness of the issues introduced above and described in depth in the following chapters. The interviews, then, supported the development of my analysis, which focused on identifying emerging themes in women's experiences of abuse and after leaving abusive partners. The themes and the relations between them form the basis of the following chapters.

Notes

1 Johnson (1989), however, argues that feminism and functionalism may not be incompatible.

2 Defining research as feminist is complex for a number of reasons, some of which are as follows. First, researchers may mask the more feminist aspect of their studies in order to publish their findings, as many publishers, particularly in America, are less likely to accept work that is explicitly feminist (Bograd, 1988; Bowker 1983). Secondly, researchers may identify themselves as feminist but not acknowledge the body of methodological discussions put forth by feminists, and thus produce studies which do not adhere to the developing feminist guidelines for conducting research. Thirdly, because feminist analysis develops and changes with time, research which may have been considered feminist in the past may seem non-feminist in the present. An example of this is Walker's work on learned helplessness, which at first was a major contribution to American feminist analysis as it attacked the myth of the masochistic woman. However, with the criticism that has been forwarded since, it has become clear that viewing battered women as 'helpless' supports the stereotype that women are passive victims. One of the major criteria I have used to define work as feminist is whether an approach acknowledges and integrates previous feminist work in its methodology and in the conclusions drawn from research results.

3 Although such factors may not be the sole reason that women are abused by their partners, the legal system which does not protect the rights of battered wives is symptomatic of the larger context of patriarchal control over women. Thus legislation and the legal response to batterers must be changed, in addition to the gender hierarchy which gave rise to the legacy of legislation surrounding battering, if woman battering is to end.

4 Within the discipline of sociological research, Dobash and Dobash's study did not go unchallenged. In a review by Richard Gelles (1979) of their work, he proposed that 'While the ideology of *Violence against Wives* is attractive and persuasive, the logic and science of the presentation are flawed, narrow, and often naïve.' Furthermore, he criticized the lack of a comparison group within the study, which he expressed as a severe deficiency in research methodology. However, one reason the methodology of Dobash and Dobash's study did not strictly conform to the popular sociological methods of the 1970s is that they were proposing a new approach which they felt could reveal more than that allowed by traditional methods (Dobash and Dobash, 1981).

5 Although Gelles was critical of Dobash and Dobash's study at the time of its publication, he has more recently recognized the contribution of gender inequality to the problem of woman battering. Although his primary focus still remains on the family dynamics which he proposes underlie abuse, he recently called for prevention strategies which included the stipulation that:

> The entire mental health movement must join hands with the women's movement and seek the elimination of our culture of sexism. Feminism is directly beneficial to the physical and mental health of all members of our society. (Gelles and Straus, 1988: 203)

Although it is not clear what exactly Gelles is referring to when he uses the words 'feminist' and 'elimination of sexism', or how such a goal could be realized, clearly feminist work has become of such importance that it can no longer be ignored or discounted by traditional researchers.

6 The literature on lesbian violence has been produced almost entirely by the American battered women's movement and is not in general very accessible. All the information I have used, apart from Lobel and NiCarthy's published work, is from the collection belonging to a Los Angeles shelter. Information on the issue may be available through the organization WOMAN, Inc. (2940 16th Street, San Francisco, CA 94103,

USA) which, at the time of this research, offered reading materials. Also, in Britain, Kelly and WAFE have begun to address the issue (Kelly et al., 1989; Kelly, 1991; WAFE, 1990).

7 An extreme example of the court system acting on the myth that 'women ask for it' is the American case in which a judge gave a 90 day sentence on a work-release programme to a man who had sexually assaulted a five year old girl. The judge explained that because the girl was 'an unusually sexually promiscuous young lady' her assailant could not have 'initiated sexual contact' but rather simply 'did not know enough to refuse' (*Columbus Citizen-Journal*, in Richardson and Taylor, 1983: 171).

8 This perspective can be particularly ironic when it is reflected in the responses of others to battered women. Claudette McShane (1988) gives an example of a woman who was assaulted by a dating partner. 'She tried for help first from the police but help was denied because they weren't married' (p. 63). It would seem that the current focus on marital violence is producing a circumstance in which other forms of violence against women carried out by intimates is not seen as woman battering.

9 Moreover, Amy Edgington provides one of the few suggestions made by the feminist and lesbian community about how lesbian battering serves the same role as abuse in heterosexual relationships in supporting women subordination. From personal experience, she suggests that the impact of her partner's abuse shattered her belief in the common perception of the time that women did not commit violence or abuse in the same manner or to the same degree as men. Consequently, she experienced a deep distrust of women in her community in general which diminished her involvement in campaigns against heterosexism. She writes:

> the struggle for sisterhood scares the hell out of me. This could be the most far-reaching damage done by Lesbian battering: it has caused many highly political, hard-working, caring Lesbians to not want to get within ten feet of a meeting [or] support group . . . Battered Lesbians are those women whose faces you never see anymore, who dropped out of politics . . . The experience of being battered by my lover did more to feed my internalized homophobia than a lifetime of conditioning by straight society. This should provide a clue to those who are still scratching their heads and asking how Lesbian battering could possibly serve the patriarchy. (Edgington, 1988: 9, 21)

10 I apply the American common use of the term 'black' to refer to African Americans. This is distinct from the British use of the term to apply to women of colour from many different cultures and races.

11 Although in the theoretical literature the experiences of battered women of colour are scarce, the issue of understanding the needs of battered women of colour is fairly well acknowledged within the American battered women's movement. This acknowledgement was made necessary by the high use of shelter facilities by low income women, which includes many black women. Also, in Britain, the Southall Black Sisters have been influential in national campaigns and coalitions in advocating for the development of services for specific ethnic groups.

12 A diverse collection of the experience of battered women of colour in America is entitled *The Speaking Profits Us: Violence in the Lives of Women of Color* (Center for the Prevention of Sexual and Domestic Violence, 1986). It includes essays on the experience of black, Asian, native American and Hispanic women and is available from the Center at 1914 N. 34th Street, no. 105, Seattle, WA 98103, USA. In Britain, *Against the Grain: a Celebration of Survival and Struggle* (Southall Black Sisters, 1990) documents issues facing women in Britain.

13 However, the extent to which refuges can offer skills to overcome the powerlessness of refuge residents when dealing with a patriarchal social structure is limited (Pahl, 1985a; Schechter, 1982). For example, Pahl (1985a) also investigated the extent to which refuges are effective in putting their ideology into successful action. The NWAF has explored ways in which battered women residents can be involved in the decision-making process of a refuge in order to share the power of refuge organization and to reinforce the decision-making capabilities of refuge residents (Pahl, 1985b). However, the results of Pahl's study are inconclusive with regard to the impact of collective decision-making of refuge residents, and her study is limited to women's experiences of one particular refuge.

14 Harding (1981) distinguishes three elements of 'feminist methodologies': the actual techniques or 'methods' used in conducting research; the theory and analysis of research, or 'methodology'; and the epistemology of research. Also see *Breaking Out: Feminist Consciousness and Feminist Research* for a fuller exploration of issues in producing feminist research (Stanley and Wise, 1983a). In addition, other issues have been raised in the anthologies by Bowles and Klein (1983) and Roberts (1981).

15 One US shelter for which I voluntarily worked actively used the following definition of domestic violence: 'An increasingly severe pattern of verbal and/or physical abuse designed to instil fear and control behaviour without any regard to the victim's rights.' This definition, then, focuses on the fear and sense of control experienced by women and accepts that these feelings may result from either physical or verbal abuse or both. Thus, women who were threatened by their partners could be accepted by the shelter without having to endure the physical damage which usually forms the basis of defining 'battered women'.

16 Luckily this woman felt clear enough about the effect of the interview that she recognized a need to decline further discussion and surround herself with an environment in which she could cope with this new surge of emotions.

17 Egan, for example, suggests that there are three stages to a helping relationship in which a helper or counsellor facilitates a client in learning to manage human problems. These stages are: exploration, new understanding and action. In the first stage, critical skills for facilitating a client's exploration of her problems are: attention giving; listening; communicating empathic understanding, non-critical acceptance and genuineness; paraphrasing by reflecting feelings, summarizing and helping the client to be specific (Egan, 1982). These are the very skills identified by Whyte (1982) to be similar to those used in interviewing, and are the prominent kinds of responses I made during the interviews.

3

Women's Experiences of Emotional Abuse

Central to much of the literature on 'battered women' is a wealth of description about specific forms and degrees of abuse. What has arisen from past research knowledge is that women can suffer from a horrific degree of mutilation and physical damage as a result of their partners' behaviour, (Dobash and Dobash, 1978; Pagelow, 1981a; Roy, 1977; Steinmetz, 1977b; Straus, 1980; Walker, 1979a).

Like the subjects of these studies, the women I interviewed described incidents of brutal violence which confirmed the findings of other work. This included the focus on the possessiveness of abusers (Dobash and Dobash, 1980) and the kinds and degree of physical abuse which is enacted (Dobash and Dobash, 1980; Gelles, 1974; Lobel, 1986; D. Martin, 1978; Pagelow, 1981b; Walker 1979a). Specifically, women in my and other studies described incidents in which one distinct form of assault was committed, such as being slapped across the face, hit with a fist, or violently pushed to the ground, against furniture or against a wall. Over time, assaults became more prolonged and brutal.

Furthermore, I want to emphasize that, because of the similarities between the experiences of lesbian and heterosexual women,[1] I have not attempted to separate out lesbian abuse as a distinct category of abuse. Lesbians' experiences of both physical and emotional coercion illustrate the general concepts of women's experience discussed in this thesis and, in any case, the number of lesbian women included in this study is too small to draw any general conclusions. Thus only when their experiences differ from those of heterosexual women, such as their descriptions of the impact of homophobia on their identification of abuse and the process of leaving, is their identity as lesbians of relevance. Others have begun to identify how lesbian abuse differs from that experienced by heterosexual women. For example, Barbara Hart points out that one way in which lesbians are coerced by their partners is through the threat that they will expose their sexual orientation to family, employers etc. (Hart, 1986). I address their experience as abused *lesbians* rather than abused *women* only when this distinction sheds light on a particular difference or when there is a specific need to clarify that both heterosexual and lesbian women had similar experiences. The same holds true for any subgroup of women who have one particular aspect of their relationship in common, such as women not married to their abusers, women of a specific race or ethnic identity, and women from a particular economic background or status. Thus, women's experience of physical violence in my work was not greatly different from that described in the vast amount of research that has been carried out on 'battered women'. What *did* strike me as new was the information women offered about their experience of emotional abuse. In the experience of the women I interviewed, emotional abuse seemed to be a deeper and more central form of abuse, particularly in relation to women's experiences of abuse and of leaving their abusers. There is some hint, in recent feminist work, of the existence and depth of 'emotional' or 'mental' abuse (Ferraro, 1979; NiCarthy, 1986; NWAF, 1977; 1979; Yllö and Bograd, 1988).[2]

Also, the effect of psychological invasion and physical pain or disability resulting from physical violence alters women's perspectives and sense of control, and thus contributes to women's experience of 'emotional abuse'. The following passage shows how, in relationships with a physically abusive partner, the emotional and physical aspects of abuse are inextricably linked:

> I used to say I found the *verbal* abuse much worse than the physical abuse. Even though the physical abuse was terrible. Because I suppose it was only – only!? God – once, twice a year. It was the constant verbal barracking that used to get me down more than anything. Cause *that's* how you lose your self-esteem. But the violence is awful, the violence is terrible. I think you've got to take that, though, as part of it. If you're constantly being told you are a useless jerk, to be thumped just . . . compounds it.

What is suggested in this passage is a theme which underlay all women's descriptions of physical assault – that there is a fundamental relation between emotional and physical abuse. First, there is a level of abuse which is enacted on a purely emotional level, that is 'constant verbal barracking', which has an intense impact on women and their psychological state. Secondly, there is an emotional impact in the enactment of physical abuse, and the sense that this aspect of physical abuse reinforces or 'compounds' the impact of abuse enacted on an emotional level. Thirdly, emotional abuse lays the foundation, within the psychological state of an abused woman, for the way in which she interprets the physical violence which is committed by her partner. For many women in this study, like the woman above, the emotional message carried in violence was that they, as individuals, were of desperately low human value, that they were 'useless'. Thus, although women were usually shocked by the physical nature of a first attack, such attacks carried meanings that were already familiar to them.[3]

The centrality of the theme of emotional abuse was also borne out in the women's experiences after their relationships had ended. It is evident from the interviews that recovery from emotional abuse was far more integral to the women's experiences than was recovery from physical abuse. The components and impact of emotional abuse described in this chapter were key issues for women's processes of uncovering and healing the damage abuse had wrought. In addition, within this latter aspect of their experiences, women who had suffered purely from emotional abuse described healing processes which were indistinguishable, in many ways, from those of women who had also suffered physical violence.

In this chapter I explore the question 'What is emotional abuse?' This will be followed, in Chapter 4, by an analysis of how emotional abuse is related to the dynamics of control which existed in the women's relationships.

Defining Emotional Abuse

One of the most straightforward attempts at a definition of emotional abuse comes from NiCarthy in the second edition of her book *Getting Free*:

> When *Getting Free* was written I was still struggling, as were many women subjected to emotional abuse, to identify it in specific terms. We were searching for ways to delineate it from the ordinary irritability and occasional name-calling that most couples engage in from time to time. In fact, much of that behaviour is abusive, but it may not be permanently damaging until it reaches the level of a campaign to reduce the partner's sense of self-worth and to maintain control. (1986: 285)

The confusion to which NiCarthy refers in describing the nature of emotional abuse highlights a number of issues with which I struggled.

I recognized that emotional abuse could not be categorized and quantified as can physical slaps or kicks. Likewise, the injuries that resulted could not be discussed in terms of degree, or even permanency. For, although sometimes emotional abuse can lead to suicidal thoughts or actions and so, like physical abuse, has the potential to be permanently damaging, women also described, as we will see in Chapter 7, how they transformed their emotional injury through healing. These women were reluctant to identify themselves in terms like 'permanently damaged', which suggests the existence of an impairment or flaw. Because of these complexities, like NiCarthy I struggled with naming the aspects of emotional abuse which were similar between the women's experiences, but which also were not grounded in easily observable and measurable indicators.

However, there were components of women's subjective experience which were strikingly common to women with diverse experiences. This commonality guided my approach to describing the fabric of emotional abuse. The components or elements of emotional abuse described below are drawn from experiences of abuse as defined by the women themselves, rather than from a definition of the specific abuser behaviour which underlies the enactment of emotional abuse.[4] Following an outline of components, I will explore how emotional abuse can be conceptualized as a 'web', in which interweaving of the components lends strength to the impact of emotional abuse on the women.

Identifying Emotional Abuse Through Women's Responses to It

Abuse, whether it was physical violence, sexual coercion or verbal attacks, had an impact at an emotional level which women described as deeply injurious. Thus there were two aspects of emotional abuse: the effect of physical abuse on women's emotional state, and a type of abuse that is enacted at a purely emotional level, such as verbal insults and emotional deprivation. Both of these aspects of emotional abuse were qualitatively similar in terms of the impact they had on the women. I identified six major components of women's subjective experiences to being abused. I drew heavily from the groundwork laid by NiCarthy (1986) in her description of emotional abuse. However, I have altered her components somewhat to reflect women's experiences of, rather than the acts of, abuse and to explore at greater depth the mechanisms through which this abuse has its impact. These components provide a core description of the nature of emotional abuse.

The following six components are separated for analysis although, in the lived experience of women, there was enormous overlap and interconnectedness between them. I will address this interconnection in the final section of this chapter.

Degradation
Degradation is the perception that, as a human being, one is markedly less valued or even acceptable than others. It is a sense that there is something inherent and essential about oneself that is soiled.[5] Degradation causes feelings of deep pain and sickening shame about oneself. All the women in the research felt degraded by aspects of their partners' behaviour. They described a variety of behaviours which included being continually told they were stupid, ugly, inadequate mothers, inadequate sexually, and incompetent. In addition, non-verbal forms of degradation included being forced unwillingly to perform sexual acts and repeated exhibition by the abuser of flatulence or urination. All of these behaviours carried a message of degradation for women.

Degradation, because it was essentially a transformation of women's self-value, was most potent when it was enacted through a point of personal vulnerability. Abusers either used vulnerabilities already existing in women, or they exploited those that had been opened as a result of abuse. For example, one woman remarked on how her partner manipulated and attacked an already low level of confidence about her intelligence to inflict acute degradation:

> that was one of my weaknesses, believing in my own intelligence. And I would forget things, which are the kinds of things that you do on a day to day basis. And he would go around and press his nose, this sounds really silly, and he would go 'sssss' every time I forgot something, like he was letting air out of the top of my head, like I was an air-head. And he would do it about real little things to my views on world issues.

Because she felt insecure about her intelligence, she was open to the criticisms made by her abuser. She had little confidence in this aspect of herself from which to draw as a resource for rejection of or protest against his criticisms. Not only did he attack this already vulnerable, undefendable, sense of self, but he also focused on the issue of intelligence to the exclusion of all other personal characteristics. As a result, the aspects of herself in which she had more personal confidence and sense of value, for example her sensitivity and interpersonal skills, lost significance relative to her abuser's continual focus on her intellectual ability. Consequently, she had even fewer resources of confidence upon which to draw and combat his attack on her self-value. This was the mechanism of degradation. It is a process through which the vulnerabilities possessed by the women themselves are targeted and thus was an insidious and extremely injurious component of abuse.

Although the kinds of behaviours that elicited a feeling of degradation varied, the underlying stages in degradation were similar. One stage in degradation, as demonstrated in the example above, was the repeated criticism of seemingly minor aspects of women's appearance or behaviour. The constant nature of such attack set up a process in which the women were unable to keep a grasp of their own sense of worth because their abusers' perspectives were continually reasserted. One woman described the specific nature of her experience:

> [What was verbally abusive?] Well, name-calling. And picking fault in my appearance. Or even pathetic things like picking fault in the way my underarms smelt, just really ridiculously childish things. That's the thing, they're so childish that, until you realize what a state you're in, they do go – not exactly unnoticed – but just a part of the pattern of things.

This degradation, then, was a form of continual, low level criticism which, seemingly invisibly, eroded women's sense of self-value to such an extent that there was no episode in which reassertion of self-value seemed appropriate. It is noteworthy that this type of degradation could actually create a sense of vulnerability, like that existing from personal history, through which further abuse could be carried out.

A second stage in degradation involved the imposition of abusers' own values on their partners. One woman commented on how her partner's beliefs were instilled into her own perspectives of herself:

> And when he went out [with friends], right, if I used to go out [with male friends] he used to call me a slag. It made me feel awful that I should have [gone out]. And he used to look me up and down.

She felt, despite the fact that he went out with friends and that in the past she had felt fine about doing so as well, that she was awful or like a 'slag'. Indeed, if women's sense of self-worth had been eroded in the first stage, what form of resistance did they have from the kind of extreme imposition of negative values this woman described? Being looked up and down, along with potent verbal attacks, had an intense impact on this woman. She began, not only to lose her own assessment of self-value, but also to accept the values expressed by her partner which defined her as a 'slag' and a 'whore'. She described the pain of this new evaluation of herself, stressing that she felt 'awful'. Many women described a similar feeling, a sense that they were essentially dirty or soiled. When this sense becomes less and less associated with their own behaviour and more associated with that of their abusers is the basis of a third stage in degradation.

The women described how, over time, they began to experience their worth to be determined almost entirely by the behaviour of their abusers. Once this stage was reached, degradation was extremely powerful and painful; women felt they had no opportunity to redefine a more positive self-worth because definition lay solely in the behaviour of their abusers. This form of degradation was most vividly expressed by women who had been sexually abused by their partners. One woman described how humiliated she felt in response to her partner's sexual coercion:

> Now and again he did things, like he found a bloke who wanted a threesome and I got thrown in at the deep end. And that was the part that I hated. And [I] hated me for actually ending up in that situation. On about five occasions . . . that was terrible.

The idea that, at such an intimate level, a partner was coercive, carried a strong emotional message to the woman: the message that her most personal levels of intimacy were open to manipulation and were not respected by the person with whom she entrusted this intimacy. The woman quoted above felt so deeply stigmatized by her experience that she had told only her closest friend, aside from the interview, about these incidents. The fact that this woman hated *herself*, a strikingly strong description for the manipulation and erosion of self-worth that resulted from her partner's behaviour, speaks about the extent to which women become dependent on the behaviour and attitudes of their partners.

Thus three stages in degradation occurred, each increasing in the amount of input an abuser had into a woman's own sense of self-worth, and each illuminating the depth at which the pain of degradation was felt. Moreover, each stage laid the foundation for establishing the next. Degradation was a component of emotional abuse because it resulted in the erosion of the women's sense of self-value and instilled in them the derogatory and devalued perspective held by their abusers.

Fear

Abused women experience anxiety about their physical and emotional safety and a sense that their bodies and selves are in danger of damage or destruction. The threat and occurrence of actual attacks bring with them an intense terror of pain and the potential for physical damage or death. The extremity and nature of physical attacks experienced by women in this study are similar to those documented in other literature (Dobash and Dobash, 1980; Lobel, 1986; Martin, 1976; Pagelow, 1981a; Walker, 1979a) and thus I will not describe them here. Moreover, the shattering of trust and physical safety that occurred with the first assault and the unpredictability and unpreventable nature of further assaults created an atmosphere of continual danger, and thus continual anxiety and fear. In some senses, this second kind of fear could become so overwhelming that women expressed an emotion documented in other research: relief in knowing that an attack was about to begin or had begun because the anxiety of waiting had ended (Walker, 1979a).

Women described the horrifying experience of their safety and future being completely under the control of someone else, not themselves. Just over half of the women said that, during a period ranging from weeks to years, they experienced a continual atmosphere of danger and anxious fear in response to their partners' behaviour.

Fundamental to this constant fear was that women could not predict when an attack would occur, the degree of the attack, or a reason for the attack. The fear that arose in response to having little or no control over one's physical safety, in one's own home, was itself emotionally abusive. One woman explained:

> the mental cruelty is a lot worse than the physical, cause, I mean with the physical you get a good batterin' or whatever and that's it. But with mental, you see he'll come in at 5 and doesn't want his tea, slap that up against the wall, and have a few drinks. 'What's the matter?', 'Nothing. You just wait, I've a good one for you.' So you sit there from half past 6, 7 o'clock onwards

thinkin' 'Oh my God.' And he'll jump quick and you'll jump cause you're
nervous and it'll just agitate him and so by half past 10, 11 o'clock when he's
well pissed, that's when the good hidin' comes. It might not be then, it might
be 2 o'clock in the morning, it might be 6 o'clock the next morning. But you
know, cause he's forewarned ya.

Although this woman lived with the explicit threat of abuser violence,
in other cases the threat was implicit. For example, women discerned
that their partners were tense or angry, and their experience told them
that a physical attack might be imminent. Even one of the women who
did not experience physical violence told how her partner's anger
always gave her the sense that she might be physically attacked. The
women's descriptions of waiting for an attack, wondering about the
intensity, searching their experience and resources for any method of
diffusing the potential violence, all constitute a type of mental and
emotional torture, and in fact their partners' behaviour has been
likened to the behaviour of captors who emotionally torture prisoners
of war (Russell, 1982).

In addition to fear about physical danger, many women described
suffering from an anxiety over their emotional safety. The threat of
destruction, on a psychological rather than a physical level, was
imminent for many. For example, changes in self-perspective resulting
from the progressing, subtle stages of degradation were frightening.
Women lacked control over an intangible, insidious process which they
could neither name nor see. Because of progressive, uncontrollable
change, women experienced a gut feeling of fear that their emotional
safety was under threat. This fear was elicited by abusers who used
purely emotional abuse as well as by those who were physically violent.

Thus, the women's experiences of fear included periodic, intense
terror in response to potentially life-threatening physical danger and
day to day anxiety about the threat and unpredictability of violence, as
well as the devastation of emotional well-being. Fear, of both physical
and psychological damage, is a component of emotional abuse because
it denies women the opportunity to lead free and healthy lives and
because it is experienced as a painful and traumatic emotional state.
Perpetual as well as periodically intense experiences of fear are abusive
and, as we will see in Chapter 6, are recurrent themes for women in
healing from abuse. As I will demonstrate in Chapter 4, another
dimension of this fear is the energy for self-preservation which
accompanies it, and which women may use to shift the dynamics of
control in their relationships.

Objectification
Objectification occurs when the behaviour of abusers indicates to
women that they are viewed as objects with no inner energy, resources,

needs, desires. There were three ways in which objectification was described by women.

One was their partners' demands that women alter their external expression of self in order to meet the needs and desires of the abusers. For example, in some cases partners demanded that women wear a certain kind or style of clothing which suited his or her idea of how that woman should look. Two women's comments exemplify this type of objectification:

> He used to like me to wear stockings and suspenders. He used to sort of tell me what to wear . . . and I didn't want to wear that. He says 'Put make-up on.'

> I wasn't allowed to get me hair cut. I wasn't allowed to wear skirts, cause men could look at me legs . . . It was like a regime really.

In both cases, the focus was on women's external appearance. What happened when women were coerced to meet these demands was that their appearance, rather than being a personal expression or choice, became dictated by the desires of their partners. Implicit in the demands was the denial of the personal individuality which women might express through appearance. In this sense, women were treated as objects, to be adjusted and conformed in order to meet the needs of the abusers.

A second way in which objectification was enacted was through manipulation of women's physical state. For example, one woman described how her partner reduced her level of functioning by enforcing a schedule of tranquillizers. Tranquillizers were used to suppress the reactions of the woman to abuse, and thus suppress her expression of self and render her more like an object:

> That's what it was really . . . I was supposed to be just what he wanted and he could dominate me if he tranquillized me . . . It's a way of getting your own way I suppose.

Thus in order to 'get his own way' this woman's husband used tranquillizers which effectively reduced her energy to express and demand that her own needs[6] and wishes be acknowledged. Again, the abuser's needs and wishes were to the fore, and there was denial of any held by the woman. The fact that this woman was physically incapacitated from expressing or even acknowledging her own needs was a potent demonstration of the intensity at which objectification can be enacted.

Finally, acute possessiveness also carried a message of objectification. Jealousy, the restriction of women's social contacts and the invasion of women's space outside the relationship all suggested that the women were the property of their partners. Because one cannot be property without being rendered an object capable of being owned, possessiveness is a form of objectification:

> He would just show up at my work – he did this a lot. I used to work graveyard shift, in the middle of the night he'd just be there, accusing me: 'Oh you're flirting with him, he likes you.'

This example details two aspects of possessiveness. First, the abuser assumed the right to unexpectedly appear at the woman's place of work in order to discover information about her behaviour at work. In doing so, he ignored her right and potential need for privacy, and assumed that she had no claim for requesting that her work life was not invaded. Secondly, the abuser did not merely observe her behaviour, he accused her. The accusations this woman described suggest that the abuser assumed he had the right to demand that she behave in a certain way and that, if she did not, she was deserving of accusation or reprimand. Both of these behaviours enact possessiveness because they manipulate women's relations with others and enforce sole control over women's social relations. The curtailing of social relations objectifies women because it ignores their human need for diverse and enriched social contact.

The component objectification is also significant in its relation to more general analyses of the exploitation of women. Feminists have pointed out repeatedly that one element of male control is exerted through transforming women into objects. The transformation of women into sexual objects in pornography is an example of this (Dworkin, 1981; Griffin, 1981) and theorists have argued that, in rendering women objects, men manifest their desire to wield complete control over women. I make this point to suggest that there is a fundamental connection between objectification found in emotional abuse and that identified by feminists as a mechanism of exploiting women. Although in-depth analysis of this possible connection is beyond the scope of this study, I suggest that abusers are likely to take on the modes of exploitation that are made readily available to them from the gender hierarchy existing in their culture, one of them being objectification. Like arguments about the relationship between pornography and rape (Dworkin, 1981; McKinnon, 1992), the culturally adopted modes of exploiting women through objectification may support and lay a foundation for this component or emotional abuse in intimate relationships.

In sum, I have discussed three ways in which women were treated as objects. In response, women commonly felt objectified, that they were less than human. They had less and less of a sense of their right to be treated as human beings worthy of respect, privacy and self-expression. Thus, objectification removed women from a sense of themselves as humans, and engendered the pain associated with such fundamental estrangement.

Deprivation

A common experience among the women interviewed was a feeling of deprivation as a result of the demands and controlling behaviour of their partners. Deprivation, from the perspective of women, arose from a conflict between basic human needs and an inability to meet these needs through the resources available. It was experienced as a painful feeling of constant unfulfilled need. Women spoke of both economic and social deprivation, as two prevalent forms of this abuse.

In economic deprivation, abusers assumed the right to use or allocate household income solely according to their wishes. Women spoke of being unable to purchase the food they needed and often, in order to feed the children, they went hungry. Thus physical deprivation can be enacted through withholding money. Moreover, an emotional impact of this was the stress which women described as central to their day to day lives. One woman spoke of working simultaneously at three jobs in order to earn enough to support her family and her husband's expenditures. Others spoke of losing sleep, of being unable to relax because they did not know if they and the children would go hungry from week to week, or if the electricity, phone or gas would be cut off because of unpaid bills.

In addition, economic deprivation had an emotional impact over and above the material stress it created. Women suffering from the extreme economic deprivation illustrated above described feeling a deep sense of uncertainty about the future and an inability to change circumstances such that basic needs could be met, as any effort they made for change was usually unsuccessful.

Although these women responded to constant conflict between need and the resources available in a number of creative ways,[7] such a conflict engendered a daily tension in their lives which was exhausting and debilitating. The women who struggled to pay house and food bills recalled how they continually calculated the amount of money they had and the amount of food and bills they needed to pay. They described panic at the end of the week as finances dried up and there were days ahead before receiving the next cheque. They experienced intense anxiety in shopping for food for the week because what they could afford was inadequate and poorly nutritionally balanced. One woman suffered from a difficult pregnancy because she was never able to afford the fresh food which was necessary to her health and the health of her child.

Another form of deprivation concerned women's opportunity to engage in social contact. Women's freedom for social interaction was severely curtailed by their abusers' behaviour. In some cases this was directly related to economic deprivation. The women described above also reported that they did not have the money to socialize, or obtain transport to meet friends:

> I was stuck in the house all the time. The only person I got out to see was my mother . . . he used to *say* 'you could go out', but he did it sneakily you see, he'd only give you enough money to get food and to pay the bills, and then you wouldn't have nowt left, so you *couldn't* get out.

In addition, social deprivation arose from possessiveness. Although possessiveness has been described in terms of its relation to objectification, it is also relevant to a discussion of deprivation. Women's abusers often monitor and curtail their social contacts. In most cases, the struggle to maintain friendships in the face of partners set against them is too great, and women may give up maintaining contact with friends. One woman described her experience:

> People weren't allowed to call me at all. *Nobody* could call me *ever*. And if people did call me he would pick up the phone and he'd say 'she's busy, she'll call you back, she's busy!' . . . and he said 'you don't have time for friends! The only things you have time to do is study and take care of *me*, those are the only things you have time to do.' At first I'd say 'Well. I *need* friends, I need . . .' – he goes 'you don't need that! You need me.' So that was about two years we lived together and that's kinda what happened for about two years.

The impact of social deprivation is intense isolation. Women became cut off from relations with anyone but their abusers and felt extremely isolated and alone. The intensity of this isolation cannot be underestimated. All of the shame, degradation, fear, terror and deprivation had to be held inside because there was no opportunity to develop the intimacy with others they needed in order to discuss their circumstances and feelings. They had no one who could give them an outsider's perspective on the abuse they experienced. As a consequence, their pain was intensified through isolation, and their partners were ensured protection from the influences of others who might help women see the cause of their circumstances more clearly. In this sense, deprivation constitutes an integral element of emotional abuse.

Overburden of Responsibility
This component of emotional abuse was one of the most subtle and difficult to identify for women who experienced it. Overburdening was experienced by women as the expenditure of tremendous energy in the day to day emotional and practical maintenance of their relationships and family, without return of effort or energy from their partners. They

were required to take exclusive responsibility for the emotional and practical issues of their relationships. One woman described a typical example of overburdening of responsibility. She explained, over and over throughout the two interviews, that her husband acted as if he was one of the children, that there was no mutual 'give and take' in the relationship:

> But it was *geared solely* towards *him*. It was constant compensations all the time, I can remember feeling that. Even though we had two small children, we had to do it his way. Again, like having another child, like having to deal with a four year old having a temper tantrum. He *didn't* stand there and scream and shout – it was just a kind of whine, or a moan.

Nearly half of the women reported that their partners took little or no adult responsibility in their relationships. Many women were inhibited from identifying such behaviour as abusive because they thought it also might be seen as merely peculiar. Thus their descriptions were often related in bewilderment and uncertainty. However, it became apparent, after focusing on comments surrounding this concept, that the extremes exhibited by abusers in avoiding responsibility form a subtle and thus highly insidious type of emotional abuse.

A second way in which overburdening was enacted was through abusers' explicit expectations that the women would take full responsibility for shared problems and by placing blame on the women if the action they took did not meet the requirements of the abusers. Partners rejected responsibility for behaviour, holiday arrangements and finances. This dynamic underpinned a significant and continual theme in their interactions. For example, one woman explained:

> And she really couldn't take responsibility for her behaviour ... It's extreme, but it really *did* feel this way to me, if *she* was sitting next to the tea and knocked the tea over, it somehow, it could *not* be her fault. And *if* it got into a fight long enough, it would be [construed to be] *my* fault. [She'd say that] I did something that made the tea fall over. There was a lot of that.

Thus, not only did the abusers not accept responsibility for their behaviour, but this was twisted in order to shift responsibility on to the abused woman and to further emotionally undermine her.

As a result, women spoke of feeling overwhelmed by the amount of responsibility that they had been manipulated to accept. For example, one woman described how the lack of mutual 'give and take' led her to feel inexplicably weighed down such that, eventually, she became emotionally and physically unable to care for her children because of the severity of her depression. In this way, overburdening as a result of abusers' refusal to accept adult responsibility was abusive because it weighed women with such a tremendous sense of responsibility that they became, in extreme cases, immobilized and unable to function.

As with other components, this form of abuse may be particularly relevant to the social context of women's subordination. Carol Gilligan argues that women's identity is developmentally grounded in their sense of being able to take responsibility for and to care for others (Gilligan, 1982). This suggests that, when this ability is exploited, the need to reject being overburdened by responsibility may conflict with the deepest roots of women's sense of identity. For this reason, this component of abuse may be particularly effective and painful in its impact on women.

Distortion of Subjective Reality

A final component of emotional abuse involved the constant shedding of doubt on women's perceptions by abusers and forceful and continual presentation of conflicting ones. Women spoke of ways in which their confidence in their perceptions about themselves, the dynamics of their relationships, and even factual information about their experiences, all of which form their subjective reality, were attacked. This type of abuse is similar to the behaviour NiCarthy calls 'crazy-making' (NiCarthy, 1986). Constant irreconcilability between what women perceived and what their partners maintained eventually led to women questioning the validity of their own subjective reality. For example, one woman commented:

> You don't have any reality base. Cause what you see is not what you're told is happening, *constantly*. It's like that whole thing with that jealousy when I *knew* I wasn't doing anything. And yet, after a while I would [think] where there's smoke there's fire – what am I doing? I must be doing something.

Eventually, her abuser's certainty of her unfaithfulness seemed so inexplicably strong that, although on the one hand she was certain of her fidelity, on the other she also began to question whether she had had sexual relations without knowing or remembering. This type of doubt about one's self-knowledge was extremely destructive to these women's emotional security. Half of the women who experienced distorted reality described a terrifying sensation in which they felt that the very foundations of their knowledge of what was real were shaken. For example:

> abuse was a *lot* like interrogation and it's a lot like being kidnapped and thrown in a closet and having somebody yell stuff to you every day. After a while the human brain just gives. I mean your *structure* just gives into it.

In having a sense of distortion and distrust of their perceptions, women felt increasingly vulnerable to their partners because of this lack of security in themselves.

Like objectification, this component of emotional abuse holds strong echoes for feminist analysis of control of women through mental health. Chesler's ground-breaking book, for example, details a history through which women have been institutionalized, depowered, and controlled by defining behaviour that threatens male power as 'madness' (Chesler, 1972). The parallels to these women's experiences are striking and, again, suggest that the cultural context in which abuse takes place may lend structure to the forms of its enactment.

An important aspect of distortion of subjective reality is its relation to women's experience of sexual abuse. Distortion of a fundamental level of subjective reality occurred for all the women in the group who had been sexually abused. In fact, this component of their experiences was so salient that often their descriptions of acts of abuse were conveyed in terms of the effect it had on their subjective realities. One woman, when asked what her partner did that she felt was abusive, described the kinds of sexual abuse that she experienced:

> He um . . . sexual things . . . he liked to hit me, he liked to tie me up, if I said no . . . if he paid any attention it was 'your lips say no, no, no but your eyes say yes, yes, yes.' . . . But he used to like to spank me until I was red, or scratch me until there were marks.

Although she related a number of physical acts of abuse, she returned again and again to the deep distortion of subjective reality that accompanied abuse on such an intimate level. Being told that she wanted the abuse enacted against her touched a basic level of confidence about her own perceptions of herself.

This woman, and the others who experienced sexual abuse, described a sense of unreality which dominated their lives over the period that they were abused. The distortion was so profound that women also felt horror, as if their lives and perspectives about the world were unpreventably becoming a sickening caricature of what they once believed. One woman gave a vivid description:

> I was sinking into a real surreal existence. And I used to look a lot at the paintings of surrealist artists because I felt that's what my *life* was turning into.

The estrangement from the reliability of her own perceptions and her lack of control over this loss could only be mitigated by submergence in an art that reflected her sense of distortion. Thus, experiencing a distortion of or confusion about subjective reality was a theme described by a number of the women interviewed, but it was particularly predominant in the experiences of women who had been sexually abused by their partners.

This, then, is the sixth component of abuse. Distortion of subjective reality is abusive because it shatters the women's confidence in their own perceptions. This component is abusive because it creates a lived experience of distance and separation from the external, objective world in which women live, and this disjuncture threatens the emotional and psychological well-being of abused women.

A Web of Emotional Abuse

Thus far I have described six components which comprise women's experience of emotional abuse. For analysis, these components have been identified and explored as distinct elements. However, in women's lived experience, the components are interwoven in such a way that they comprise a whole which has properties beyond merely the sum of those of individual components. To reflect this 'whole' I use the concept of a 'web'. This imagery conveys that emotional abuse, as a whole, is a network of interrelated behaviours and emotions. This network is extremely difficult to discern when women are caught within it. The concept of a 'web' also conveys the overriding sense arising from women's descriptions that they were trapped and held within a relationship that threatened to destroy their emotional and physical safety.

The analysis above describes six major components of abuse. These components comprise the basic elements of women's experience, as do the supporting strands of a 'web'. At any one time, or in any one event, a woman may feel the strength of one component. An in-depth look at one woman's experience demonstrates how components are interconnected and how such interconnections reinforce the impact of each in the whole structure of the 'web' of emotional abuse.

The woman met her partner in college and they were married for two years. They had one daughter. Her descriptions of abuse centred largely around verbal degradation, in which her partner repeatedly devalued her education and her intellect. In addition, she described sexual abuse in which her partner continually ignored her protests or asserted that she really *did* want to engage in the sexual acts to which she objected. Over time, his sexual demands grew more and more abusive. She suffered from scratches and bruises and extreme humiliation as a result of his behaviour and sexual coercion. If we look at her experience of the components of emotional abuse we begin to see how, in the lived experience, they are highly interwoven.

When initially asked about the behaviour her partner enacted that she felt was abusive, she began to describe her experience of degrading verbal assaults:

> He always put me down. I was an art major, if you're not hard science it's just not worth anything. You kinda take it with a grain of salt but if you hear it over and over and over again you start to really feel stupid, especially when it's someone you care about, who supposedly loves you. He was always telling me that I was dumb, or not as smart as other people, or that my major wasn't worth anything.

From verbal abuse, the seed of degradation was planted. Constant verbal attacks on her self-worth took their toll, and she began to really believe that she was not as intelligent as others, that her work and her achievements in college were not valuable.

At the same time as she was feeling degraded and devalued, she was also suffering from a loss of confidence in her own perceptions about his verbal attacks. At the beginning she viewed his comments to be a personal perspective but over time she no longer was able to hold on to this distancing from his abuse and began to believe his criticisms. Over time, then, her sense of subjective reality became distorted. As this process of the distortion of subjective reality took place, she became more and more vulnerable to her partner's sexual abuse and suggestions that she wanted him to behave in certain kinds of ways. Thus her partner exploited the vulnerability created through degradation to further his abuse and deepen her sense of a distorted subjective reality. In time, she described how total this distortion became:

It *was* confusing. It was like . . . *I* didn't know what was real and what wasn't. I didn't know if what I was thinking was right or not. I felt like 'well gee, I don't like anal intercourse but maybe that's *wrong*.' Cause he'd be telling me that I *should*. And he'd be telling me 'Oh yes you do like it, you do like it' and after you *hear* it so much . . . it got so I didn't know what I was, who I was, as far as I'm concerned, it wasn't *me* that was there, it wasn't the real me.

Clearly, the abuse engendered a potent experience of distorted reality. In time, she became unable to discern what was real, what was right or wrong. Again, from her description we see a connection to a third component: objectification. As she no longer felt secure in knowing what was real, she also began to feel as if she was unable to express her needs which challenged her partner's enforced perceptions of reality. Eventually, she lost the ability to acknowledge her needs and wishes almost entirely. She felt as if she had become an object upon which her partner enacted his abuse and was unable to protest at his demands. She described her eventual state: 'By that time I had been so . . . brainwashed I felt incapable of saying no.' Hence, the licence to abuse was complete, and her abuser continued his sexual abuse.

Thus at the same time this woman felt confused about her perception of subjective reality, objectified, and deeply degraded. These are three supporting strands of the web of abuse in which she was entangled. In the lived experience, they were not experienced as distinct because of the way in which they reinforced and interwove with each other. Moreover, other components also existed and supported the overall structure of the web. Both her sense of shame and her partner's active interference in her social life led her to a sense of social isolation or deprivation. This isolation had profound implications for her experience of distorted reality and loss of identity. Because over time she was less and less able to share her experience with others, she had no access to perspectives external to the relationship which might challenge her partner's behaviour towards her. Thus her isolation intensified her sense of confusion about reality.

Finally, in her experience of the web of abuse, all these components added to this woman's sense of fear. As she lost trust in her perceptions and self-value, reinforced by her lack of social contact, she increasingly perceived her partner as extremely powerful. His abuse became nearly the only form of human interaction to which she was exposed. She was extremely vulnerable to his criticisms. Not surprisingly, his presence and power began to feel overwhelming and she felt intense fear of his capabilities to control her. She described how, when making plans to escape, she was overcome with sheer terror about the capacity of her partner to manipulate and prevent her:

> Panic, panic. Panic because I didn't know if I could do it. Panic because I thought he could change my mind. Panic because I was *sure* he would know what I was thinking . . . that he'll know something has changed in me. So panic that I wouldn't be able to get away.

In this passage it is clear that the impact of her abuser's influence had assumed immense power. She was not even sure that she would be able to resist his attempts to change her mind or conceal her thoughts. She felt her partner had complete access and control over her, even to the level of her private thoughts. Although the dynamics of how this occurred and its implications for understanding abuse and control are the subject of Chapter 4, this particular example informs understanding of her sense of fear. The woman was extremely anxious about and fearful of her partner. He began to seem to hold superhuman power in her eyes, and the fear she felt in response to this power affected and complicated her attempts to leave. Although she was successful in leaving, she had to cope with the devastating effect of fear which was so potent that she nearly decided to remain in the relationship.

This is only one glimpse of the way in which the components of abuse were interconnected and, consequently, formed a web-like structure which was difficult for the women to disentangle and from which it was difficult to attain freedom. Within the interviews there were innumerable examples of the fine interlacings of the web of abuse. The terminology of 'web', then, conveys the fabric of emotional abuse with respect to its delicate interconnections, which afford an overall strength and a capacity to entrap.

Moreover, the model conveys a sense of the insidious nature of emotional abuse in that it is experienced as a subtle, nearly invisible, process through which the fundamental components of its impact are ingrained in women, and as a result their escapes are complex and painful. One woman described how the imagery implicit in this model reflects the basic nature of her experience. In the process of recovering from abuse she commented:

> It would be as if when a spider weaves a web you don't see it very clearly. It's when, it's on two trees and the sun is shining through it, there's dew on it, that you can really really *see* the outline . . . if you could take a can of spray paint and spray it so that you could see all the linking things that make it manipulative, and what it undermines, and what it's attached to, what string it pulls.

Thus, in addition to the deeply destructive components of emotional abuse, what made them powerful in keeping women trapped within a relationship with an abuser was their interconnectedness. As in a web, the components were interwoven; no one strand could be considered in isolation from the support and reinforcement of the others, and within this web, as we will see in the next chapter, the struggle for change was complex.

In looking at the intensity of the components of experience, their interrelatedness and the whole they form in terms of a web, we can understand more clearly why a focus on the discrete, measurable elements of physical abuse does not provide an adequate under-standing of abuse. NiCarthy's definition of abuse as 'a campaign to reduce the partner's sense of self-worth and to maintain control' moves towards recognition of this web. This chapter illuminates why emotional abuse is effective in maintaining control. It also clarifies how the foundations for physical abuse are laid and thus addresses some of the confused and baffling perspectives about severely victimized battered women such as described in Chapter 1.

Notes

1 Moreover, Hart's definition of lesbian battering can be applied to the experiences of two women in my study, and does not differ greatly from definitions of abuse enacted by male partners in terms of the control and authority they gain:

> Lesbian battering is the pattern of intimidation, coercion, terrorism or violence, the sum of all past acts of violence and the promises of future violence, that achieves enhanced power and control for the perpetrator over her partner. (Lobel, 1986: 174)

2 One signal that this form of abuse has begun to be noticed is that the terminology of feminist writings has shifted from a focus on the physical, implied in the word 'battered', to words which reflect the diversity of women's experiences, such as woman or wife 'abuse' (NiCarthy, 1986; NWAF, 1977; 1979; Yllö and Bograd, 1988).

3 I must stress that, although I am focusing on emotional abuse, I am not implying that the physical abuse experienced by women is of secondary importance. The horrific nature of the violence enacted on women featured in this study and in others is of great significance to understanding woman abuse. However, as this aspect has already been

documented by many researchers (see Chapter 1), I do not intend to address it at great length.

4 NiCarthy (1986) and Russell (1982) suggest categories of emotional abuse, some of which are similar to mine. However, in their analyses, Russell focuses on sexual abuse of women in marriage and NiCarthy presents her category in a non-analytical context. Although my work was informed by these sources, the categories I distinguish and discuss are intended to further the work done by NiCarthy and Russell by exploring a wide range of women's experiences and by placing them in a conceptual framework.

5 Throughout this book, I use the term 'self' to reflect women's use of it, as a name for the knowledge people hold about who they are. This includes a sense of certainty about one's experiences, skills, abilities, perceptions of the world and others, relations to others etc. However, I am aware that, in broad academic debate, the term is problematic. Discussions about the relation of self to language and social interaction have been raised by sociologists (Manis and Meltzer, 1972; Mead, 1962; Wylie, 1961). Mead (1962) argues that self arises only from social experience and that it reflects the social experience of an individual, for example. In addition, psychologists have suggested that self can refer to the entire organism in a broad definition of the word (Westen, 1985), to the drive within to fulfil needs (Maslow, 1962), or to aspects of experience which are non-social (Piaget and Inhelder, 1969; Westen, 1985).

6 Like the term 'self', 'needs' is also problematic. It can be seen in a strictly biological sense – the needs of the physical organism to maintain its existence – or defined in terms of what an individual requires to maintain an adequate and fulfilling lifestyle in addition to physical survival. I use the term in the broadest psychological sense throughout the analysis, referring to a wide range employed by psychologists which includes physical need for food and shelter, need for safety, love and esteem (Ainsworth, 1979; Bowlby, 1969; Hunt, 1965; Maslow, 1962; Westen, 1985).

7 It must be noted, however, that even when women are experiencing extreme economic deprivation, they respond with active and creative coping mechanisms. For example one woman, whose husband continually checked her purse to assess whether she could manage to pay the bills and feed the family on less than the minimal amounts he was giving her, hid away small sums of money, usually not more than a dollar, such that he would not be able to account for their absence. In this way she slowly built up an emergency fund and reduced her extreme dependence on her husband's willingness to give her the money she needed.

4

Emotional Abuse and the Dynamics of Control

The research described in Chapters 1 and 2 suggests that abuse, in the form of physical violence, affords a partner increased control over a woman (Dobash and Dobash, 1980; D. Martin, 1976; NiCarthy, 1986). In the previous chapter I have described the components and impact of the emotional abuse which coexists with the forms described in other research. What role the web of emotional abuse plays in the dynamics of control, and what women who left their partners did to break out of it, are the subject of this chapter.

Power and Control: some Basic Definitions

It is clear from the previous chapter that the women began to lose confidence in their perceptions in response to being abused, and that they became more vulnerable to the perspectives voiced or implied by their partners. In much of the literature, this effect, as it is related to physical abuse, is described in terms of women's experiences of 'powerlessness', 'helplessness' or increased abuser 'control' (Dobash and Dobash, 1980; NiCarthy, 1986; Stanko, 1985; 1987; Walker, 1979a). But what is the nature of this control or power? Based on the experiences of the women I interviewed, I have looked more closely at the meaning of power and control and how women lose and also regain sufficient power and control to allow them to leave their partners. In this context, I found the following definitions of power and control most useful.

Control by one over another exists when one person has greater influence over the other's behaviour or perspectives than does that person herself.[1] In the experiences of the women interviewed, control was enacted in both an emotional and a physical way. Emotional control occurred when women began to lose touch with their own wants, needs and perceptions and were influenced more by the demands and perspectives of their partners. Physical control occurred, for example, when women were unable to prevent attacks, slowed by tranquillizers and confined to their homes when their partners locked the doors or prevented their leaving.

Marilyn Frye (1983) suggests that we have a cultural predisposition to define coercion in terms of being physically overpowered. She argues that the manipulation of a woman's options by another person such that the most attractive choice available to her is to conform to the desire of that person is a prevalent way in which women are coerced. Yet this control of options is unacknowledged by definitions based solely on physical force. The same is true for defining control. For example, the commonly raised question of why a woman does not leave an abusive partner during periods in which she is not physically restrained defines the issue in physical terms and ignores broad dimensions of control enacted through emotional or mental means. Yet, as we will see, the type of abuse described in Chapter 3 has a very definite and effective impact on the dynamics of control.

In my analysis I have used a very simple definition of power as the sum total of personal and external resources brought to bear on the exertion of control.[2] Thus, a partner who is abusive uses his or her own powers of persuasion, his or her sensitivity to the vulnerabilities of a woman, his or her physical strength and many more personal resources to enact control. Moreover, if that partner has access to external resources, such as management of the family income, he or she can use this to enact further control, such as economic deprivation. The hierarchies of Western culture, which afford men greater resources in terms of money, cultural status and the historical legacy of men's right to 'punish' their wives, support men's abuse of women and have been revealed to be factors contributing to violence against women by men in general (Dobash and Dobash, 1980; Mazzola, 1987; Pleck, 1987). Racial hierarchies afford black women even less access to economic and judicial support. Threat of exposure of a woman's lesbian identity can silence lesbians abused by their partners in requesting support. Thus these socially constructed power relations play a role in the social phenomenon of male violence against women.

Another complexity in understanding the power dynamics of abuse within Western culture is that the use of the term 'power' evokes a tension between 'power over' and 'power to' or 'empowerment'. In current feminist literature, the former is usually used in discussion of men's relation to women within a patriarchal culture, and the latter in that of women's efforts to overcome the restriction of freedom created by patriarchal culture. Both are related to the impact of the structure of patriarchy on those living within it and both refer to the use of resources, either those socially granted or those pulled from personal sources, to maintain or change a particular power dynamic. Thus there is a tension in the term 'power' in that it is used to describe how exploitation or oppression works, and in these cases it is generally portrayed as negative. Yet it is also becoming more common in descriptions of how oppressed or exploited people challenge and make changes in the structure of oppression, and in these cases it is generally portrayed as positive and affirming. Examples of this are the phrases 'reclaiming power', 'women's power' and 'empowerment' which are part of the vocabulary of the women's and battered women's movements.

Power structure in society clearly affords male abusers more resources with which they can enact control. However, women and their partners have different relations to the concept of power which extend beyond a simple division of victim/woman as powerless and abuser/male as powerful.

Power and Control within the Dynamics of Abuse

The balance of control between women and their abusers can shift: women can experience either increased or decreased abuser control. This movement can be visualized as a spiral. Both inward and outward directions of movement described in women's stories include events or dynamics which are similar. Their stories were commonly circular in that, as they spoke chronologically of what had happened, they continually came back to core issues at different stages of the progress. Yet, when a woman moves outward along the spiral path, towards decreased abuser control, she will have a different perspective on the re-emerging issues than when she is held tightly in the centre or is being pulled inward. For example, a woman may describe returning to a relationship with an abuser after a period of separation. She may have regained hope that her partner had changed, and may have returned only to experience the same forms of subtle emotional abuse gradually transforming into physical violence. This progression of abuse may, on the surface, seem to mirror what she experienced before she left her partner. She may even feel that she has come full circle and blame herself for what seems like a repeat of the past. However, through the act of leaving, she has gained the knowledge that she can leave. If she stayed in a shelter, she will know that there are shelters and networks of support and that she is not alone. All this knowledge, plus her past history with her partner, will give her a different perspective on the progression of abuse and, despite her return, she will not be as close to the centre of the spiral as she was previously.

This conceptualization of psychological change is reflected in other literature. A downward spiral has been used to describe the way in which women descend into hopelessness within relationships with abusive partners (Proposition Two RTIC, 1992). Feminist therapists have visualized emotional healing as an upward spiral with similar analogies to those I propose (Chaplin, 1988). Thus the model is not original to this text, but its relation to the dynamics of power and control and the web of abuse, as I will discuss later in this chapter, is new.

So, as I discuss the two major shifts in movement along the spiral, and the act of leaving the spiral, I will return, as did the women in telling their own stories, to issues which have been raised previously. Inward movement is marked by the establishment of control by an abuser. As described in Chapter 3, women experienced a loss of confidence in their own perspectives and sensitivity to their needs in response to the abuse their partner enacted, and thus they were less able to behave according to their own needs and beliefs. Consequently, the abuser attained greater influence and an opportunity to impose his or her definitions, and the woman became caught in the centre of the spiral or moved inward towards increased abuser control. By beginning to identify that the relationship was having significant negative effects on their lives, women moved outward. This occurred when women understood that their sense of self-value had been shattered, when they began to question the feeling of being 'weighed down', and when they were confronted with undeniable physical changes in themselves, such as changes in health and weight. These acknowledgements were a first step in the women's efforts to look at their relationships differently and to find a way to reverse the personal damage that they had incurred. A second factor in outward movement consisted of a change in the energy level of the abused women. This factor often led to leaving an abuser. Women described a strong sense of either anger or fear, accompanied by a need for self-preservation or the protection of their children. This energy is a personal resource upon which women draw to shift the balance of control, to regain the ability to act on their own needs and wishes, and, eventually, to leave the partner who is abusing them.

The concept of a spiral simplifies in order to highlight the overall movement necessary to leave an abuser. It is essential to note that, as with the application of any model to human experience, the concept does not always encompass the full complexity and diversity of the individual, lived experience. In terms of a spiral, the chronology of inward and outward movement may be different for some women. For example, they may experience anger before they are sure what they are angry about, or they may go back and forth between identifying how the relationship has affected them and feeling overwhelmed by the effects of low self-esteem and depression. Usually, women are experiencing movement in different directions, at some level, throughout the relationship, but one may be more dominant or salient at a particular time. Women may be subject to a high degree of influence and control by their partners while, at the same time, understanding that one aspect of their abusers' behaviour has had a negative impact. For example, a woman may understand that, because of the economic deprivation her partner enforces, she is physically debilitated because she is unable to buy adequate and healthy food. She may also feel extremely angry at times because she is unable to meet her needs and the needs of her children, and eventually, if not prohibited by her abuser, she may seek employment but not leave the relationship. This action for change within the relationship is motivated by her anger and may initially afford her more economic control. Thus, within one aspect of her relationship, she may have experienced outward movement along the spiral.

However, during the same period, other aspects of her relationship may be experiencing inward movement. For example, she may not see that the social deprivation which accompanies her economic deprivation is affecting her esteem because she has no support network to affirm her worth. Over the period in which she is moving outward in relation to income, she may move inward in relation to social contact and her partner will use this relative powerlessness to maintain control. Moreover, most outward movements are accompanied by a response from abusers which serves to pull women inward. Many women, for example, spoke of how extra income they earned in their employment was eventually controlled or used by their abusers, leaving women working outside the home in addition to carrying on their household and family responsibilities with little economic reward. Thus there may be many spirals in a single woman's experience, each related to a different issue or component of abuse.

Presentation of this general concept is in no way meant to imply that all women 'should' go through these stages or that those who don't are in some way deviant from the norm. It is not meant as a tool to assess the behaviour and success of women struggling with abuse. Rather, it is meant to convey the depth of the process described by the women interviewed and to shed light on women's experiences of the dynamics of power and control.

Moreover, no one shift in position on the spiral lasts a set time. The women experienced any one shift over a period from months to five years. The time depended on the dynamics of the relationship itself, i.e. how strongly an abuser maintained control and how many or few resources women had available to shift the power imbalance.

Moving Inward: Loss of Personal Control to an Abusive Partner

The mechanisms by which abusers established greater control were embedded in women's senses of weakened self-esteem, loss of identity, decreased control over their physical state and debilitating depression related to a loss of hope. Women described these aspects of experience as central to the dynamics of control in their relationships. The categories indicate a loss of personal resources which contribute to the relative power women hold in relationships. As the women's power lessened, then so did their ability to deny their partners' control, and thus they became bound tightly to the web of abuse.

Self-Esteem

When I use the term 'self-esteem' I am referring to the degree to which, as individuals, we see ourselves as important and valuable.[3] Self-esteem is a fundamental belief in ourselves as worthy of respect, love and fair treatment from others. When our self-esteem is weakened, it is easy to believe that we may 'deserve' to be ill treated, that we are 'failures', or that we are inherently less valuable than others.

All the women expressed the view that their self-esteem was eroded as a result of the continual physical and emotional abuse by their partners. The degradation, isolation and objectification they experienced over time worked to convince them that they had little self-worth. Particularly because women felt isolated, cut off from external views about themselves and the relationship, the messages of low self-worth communicated by their partners were potent. At the time of the interviews, when women had begun to regain self-esteem, they looked back with incredulity at the low worth their partners convinced them to hold about themselves. For example, one woman commented:

> And I can't believe those words came out of my mouth but I really really meant it . . . when I told him 'I don't even care that you hit me, just don't leave me.' I think that's really sad.

Such retrospective self-examination testifies to the depth to which women feel their self-esteem has been shattered within the relationship. Similarly, other women remarked that their self-esteem was severely damaged when they were in the relationship, but, as implied by their amazement in looking back at their feelings, they clearly began to rebuild esteem after the relationships ended. This suggests that low esteem was central to the dynamics of the relationship itself.

So, how does esteem relate to control? Fundamentally, feelings of worthlessness that arose from relationships with abusive partners reinforced women's sense that they should accept the abuse. The abuse itself, then, brought about psychological responses in women which enabled an abuser to continue or even worsen his or her behaviour. Other researchers have also identified loss of self-esteem as a common effect of physical abuse on women, and have described how it contributes to the reasons why a woman stays in a relationship with an abuser (Dobash and Dobash, 1978; NiCarthy, 1986; Prescott and Letko, 1977).

Self-esteem was one personal resource upon which women might have drawn to re-establish their power and defend themselves against the emotional impact of abuse. When women could not draw upon the resource of esteem to insist that they did not deserve abuse, they had less power because they did not have access to this resource and thus abusers were afforded the opportunity to exert more control. For example, one interviewee described how her abuser continually criticized her friends and interrupted or forcibly discontinued conversations she had with friends. Over time, as she coped with this behaviour by allowing herself to lose contact with friends, she also began to lose her sense of self-esteem, because of the emotional and physical abuse she suffered. The combination of the two left her with little opportunity for or sense of importance about maintaining friendships she had previously enjoyed. Her partner used this circumstance to focus her attention, time and behaviour on him. He began to assert that she didn't need friends, that 'the only thing she needed was him', and he began to demand all of her time and skills in helping him with his work for college. She had no internal sense of worth which would help her combat this assertion and, for a period, her partner gained nearly total control over her actions, attentions and energy.

Thus 'esteem' is one personal resource which was minimized by abuse, and the resulting reduction in power afforded the opportunity for abusers to exert further control. In the same way, loss of identity, physical disability and depression were key elements in the power dynamics of abuse.

Loss of Identity
Related to a drop in self-esteem was a sense of weakened identity described by the women interviewed. While esteem pertains to the value a person attributes to herself, identity is based on the knowledge held by a person about their personal characteristics, perspectives and values.[4] Identity, then, in some ways is even more fundamental than esteem: we can know our identity yet consider it to be low in value, but when our sense of identity weakens it is almost impossible to assess its value.

Again, women's references to their sense of weakened identity were central to their stories and, like esteem, were related with a sense of retrospective amazement. As women became confused by the constant degradation and objectification, they felt that they no longer were able to identify who they were. They were isolated from external experiences which would clarify and affirm their sense of self. As a result, one third of the women expressed a sense that they had no identity. For example, one woman described a feeling of emptiness or hollowness in relation to her sense of herself:

> And I had lost all – I'm a pretty strong personality – but I had lost all sense of myself. I would just sit on the couch in a little ball and moan, not able to move.

As they were rendered unable to draw upon the personal resource of identity they lost greater power in the relationship.

In order to consider establishing an independent life they would have had to draw upon the skills and abilities that they possessed and that formed part of their identity. But the women no longer had access to this knowledge about themselves because they no longer held a strong sense of identity or they believed their identity did not include such skills and abilities.

This loss was extremely subtle; women often related their experiences with a sense of confusion and uncertainty, indicating how complex the process of losing identity could be. It is also important to remember that these power dynamics were occurring within the confusing and frightening web of emotional abuse and were often enforced with physical violence. What I am describing are the subtleties of women's lived experience of abuse, not a psychological explanation of 'why women stay'. What is addressed here takes place in the context of a much wider set of social conditions which contribute to the complexity of leaving an abuser (Dobash and Dobash, 1980; Hoff, 1990; Marin, 1985; D. Martin, 1976; 1978; Pahl, 1985b).

Physical Ability
A third personal resource which is of importance in the dynamics of control is women's physical ability. Impairment of health, due to changes in weight and stress in response to abuse, rendered women less able to leave their partners and, in this way, reduced the power held by women and afforded greater control by the abusers.

One-third of the women stressed that their weight or health seriously changed over the course of the relationship owing to their emotional abuse and their emotional response to violence. Five of these women described a gain in weight due to compulsive eating or a change in eating patterns as a way of coping with the anxiety produced by the abusive relationship. For example, one woman stated:

> Of course when he went to work I used to sit and eat. I'd cleaned up within an hour. I used to just sit and eat crisps and chocolate. Just cause it was there, it was like a comfort . . . I was happy in myself eatin' sweets and that was the way I reacted to it.

A separate fifth of the women lost a significant amount of weight during the relationship because they could not bring themselves to eat when under the stress of living with their partners. They described how their stomachs were constantly knotted with tension because they were worried about such problems as the potential of violence, or surviving on a minimal income:

> I never used to eat, at all, nothin'. Because I was that busy waitin' for his to go up the wall, or slapped in the face with them, I could not eat.

And finally, one-fifth of the women noted that their health had changed significantly as a response to the stress of abuse. The kinds of tensions described above which contributed to over- or undereating also took their toll on the physical health of women. For example, women described chronic illnesses, a higher susceptibility to infections, and loss of hair. These were all stress reactions to the extreme daily tension of being in a relationship with an abuser:

> I didn't know how to get out of the situation for a while. And I didn't know how to offload . . . and so I was sort of trapped in this downward spiral, which culminated in me getting stomach ulcers and bowel syndrome. I was physically ill because I couldn't handle the situation. I lost a lot of weight as well, literally got down to 5 stone.

Physical debilitation impaired the women's ability to change their circumstances. Such debilitation drained them of the mental and emotional energy required to contemplate avenues of change. For example, the woman quoted above was preoccupied with the physical symptoms of her distress. Her attention focused on relieving the pain she endured and trying to survive from day to day. In this state, she had minimal physical and mental strength to free herself from her abuser, and he was able to enact more control. He did this by continually demanding her time and support. He would force her to stay up all night listening to him speak of his fears and emotional distress. Eventually, her life totally revolved around him. She lost sleep, suffered in her work, and became numb to her own needs as he dominated her time and energy. Thus, in general, an abuser may be afforded increased control or influence over a woman's behaviours and perspectives, because the abused woman is unable to summon the energy to challenge the dynamics of the relationship, as a result of the damage to her health resulting from the abuse itself.

Loss of Hope and Depression

A fourth area of personal resource which was central to the dynamics of control and power was women's experience of depression. Depression, in the context of this study, was spoken of in terms of the loss of hope that women could change the circumstances in their lives that were damaging.[5]

All the women interviewed felt that, at some point, they became depressed about their relationship with their abuser. However, depending on the degree to which women felt that their circumstances were unbearable and unchangeable, the severity of the depression varied. One-third of them felt that their circumstances were so extreme that the depression they suffered rendered them suicidal:

> In the last 6 months of the relationship I got into a (state) where – it wasn't suicidal – yet if I walked across the street and a car hit me it really didn't matter to me. It really didn't matter. It just seemed like there was no way out except to die.

> I nearly committed suicide as well. I walked out of the house one Sunday and nearly walked underneath a car.

For these women, depression rendered them unable to contemplate and seek a way of changing their circumstances, so that their vulnerability to abuser control was immense. For example, one woman described how her partner used her depression to gain increased control over her by threatening to commit her to a mental institution:

> And whatever I said, was wrong: 'You're mistaken.' And he'd think of something else, and I think he was playing up to get on my nerves . . . he said as a verbal attack 'I know what I'll do, I'll put you in R . . . that's the mental hospital for depressives.'

In this case, the depression the woman suffered in response to abuse allowed her partner to assume greater influence over her perceptions. He used the threat of institutionalization to convince her that her depression was an indication of psychological illness, rather than a response to abuse. In this way, he began to gain control over her perceptions of herself. Moreover, her partner was able to enforce his own perceptions by threatening institutionalization if she did not comply with his ideas and whims. For example, if she did not clean the house in a particular way, he would assert that she was mentally unstable and that he was going to have her 'locked up'. In order to cope with his threats, this woman began to focus more and more on meeting the needs and wishes of her abuser and less and less on her own needs, simply to avoid the possibility of being institutionalized. Her husband gained more influence not only over her perceptions but also over her behaviour, and thus gained increased control. In this way, part of the techniques that promoted women's ability to cope from day to day contributed to the amount of control abusers had over women. Such coping techniques or 'survival skills' have been documented by others (Bowker, 1983; Ferraro, 1983; Ferraro and Johnson, 1983; Finn, 1985; Hoff, 1990; Kelly, 1988b; Romero, 1985).

In sum, the above four key elements in abusers' establishment of control over women are highly interrelated, much like the 'web' of emotional abuse described previously. One woman commented on the complexity of this dynamic of control:

The thing about violence is that it isn't just the physical violence, it's the mental and sexual abuse as well . . . it's degradin', it's demoralizin', it takes away every bit of confidence as well as you're not physically on top. So if you're physically not on top and you're certainly mentally not on top, then you haven't got the strength to go around fightin' your cause yourself.

In other words, the use of emotional abuse and physical violence acted to reduce the resources on which a woman might draw to challenge her partner's control or leave an abusive partner. As is apparent from the discussion of the insidious and subtle nature of emotional abuse, this loss of power is less to do with women 'giving up' their power, a perspective which blames the women for this dynamic, and more related to the highly effective and targeted behaviour of an abuser who is intent on reducing it.

Moving Outward: Regaining Personal Control

Awareness of Personal Change within the Relationship
Both the gradual nature of the turn described above, and the intensity of the relationship in which women's attention is focused on their abusers and not themselves, obscure awareness of the magnitude of the changes that occur. This is not to say that women simply don't notice when their partners, for example, insist that they not see their friends. But what they may not see as this occurs repeatedly, with gradually increasing success, is that they are becoming completely isolated from any contact outside the relationship which might clue them in to the increasing control their partner is gaining. What they may not see is that social deprivation is undercutting their sense of self-value and self-assurance. In this way, their awareness of the personal changes that are taking place as a result of abuse may be minimal, simply because they are preoccupied with day to day matters regarding their partners' behaviour.

In this respect, when women began to gain an awareness of the personal changes that occurred within themselves, they were able to draw upon a new factor for outward movement along the spiral of power dynamics in their relationships. There are two types of awareness included in this factor that emerged. One surfaced when women began to see that they or their children had changed significantly over time and in ways which they considered to be negative. A second was uncovered when they began to question why such change was occurring and became aware of the linkages between their partners' behaviour and its impact.

Within the relationship, the women did not generally define their partners' behaviour as emotionally abusive. This occurred after they left their relationships and were able to explore their experiences without the stress of surviving abuse from day to day. Yet, there were elements of abuse that some women began to recognize within their relationships. Moreover, it is also important to note that awareness was a process in which women struggled continually with a growing sense that 'something was wrong' with the circumstances in which they lived. They repeatedly moved back and forth between different types of awareness depending on how much opportunity they had to contemplate their lives. For example, a woman may begin to see that she has few friends and that she misses them, and starts to remember all the times her partner made interaction with friends difficult or painful. If this insight is then followed by a period in which her partner becomes more violent, or threatens violence with greater frequency, particularly if this is done by the abuser to re-establish control and interfere with her efforts for renewed friendships, then she is likely to become preoccupied with new levels of fear and coping. The loss of her friendships becomes an issue that is secondary to her physical survival. During this period she is likely to think very little about the insights she had and, even if the relationship then enters a period of relative calm, she may have forgotten her realizations because of the intensity of the intervening period. In this way, women constantly moved in and out of awareness. It was a process in which they slowly built up their knowledge about the nature of the relationship and its impact. In the experience of the women interviewed, this process lasted for months or years, depending on whether the exercising of abuser control gained in the earlier phase denied them the time and attention required to become aware. In this way, as we will see, awareness was an issue central to the dynamics of control.

Awareness of Changes in Self and Children   In this type of awareness, women gained insight into the fact that they or their children had changed significantly and in negative ways. Insight of this kind usually required that women were confronted with an example of personal change which was so dramatic that they were jarred into realization. There are two ways in which this occurred. First, a vivid memory of their past confidence, perspectives or feelings served, for some, as a comparison for their current state. Second, others were faced with a nearly total inability to function or make decisions which moved them to wonder why.

Most of the women interviewed were struck at some point by comparisons between their current state and their memories of themselves before the relationship began. For example, some women, bored with staying at home every evening, suddenly remembered how they used to go out at night with friends and how much they enjoyed such contact and interaction. This memory contrasted strongly with their later attitude to social contact which they saw as something fearful and to be avoided. Although at the time they may not have made the connection between this fear and the aggressive intervention enacted by their partners towards friendships, they did realize that something dramatic had changed. A memory or confrontation which reminded women of the past shed light on the nature of their current circumstances and suggested to them that they had undergone significant, negative change.

Similarly, women spoke of becoming immobilized, of being unable to function at the type of work which they had done previously with enthusiasm and success. In these cases, it was not so much a comparison with the past that triggered their insight, but rather the problem of being confronted with work and challenges at which they did not feel they could succeed. For example, one woman spoke of how she had always been skilful at writing and public speaking on behalf of a particular organization. Such work became part of her role within the organization. When, as a result of abuse, she felt frightened or unconfident she was faced with the task of continuing this type of work despite her misgivings. The tension arising from feeling unable to do such work, and unable to explain why, gave her the opportunity to recognize the personal change. She described this experience in the following way:

> Towards the end of the relationship I began to also feel inadequate in my intellectual or political world as well. And that was one of the things that started to clue me into the fact that I had changed and that something was wrong. I started to doubt that I could do things that I can do. I started to doubt that I can write, I started to doubt that I can speak. Sometimes it would happen that the doubt would paralyse me, like I would have an article to write for a newspaper or something and I wouldn't be able to do it.

In this way, lack of the ability to function, juxtaposed against a vivid reminder of a past with more positive self-attitudes and perspectives, triggered insight into how much a woman had changed.

Thus, whether it was a contrast with the past or a sense of immobilization in the present, the realization that they had changed was significant because it planted the seed of knowledge that circumstances had to be questioned. Even in relationships in which physical abuse was severe, women felt the emotional effects were the most devastating; physical abuse may not have been a significant factor in recognizing the need for change. Instead, realization that deep personal damage had occurred was central to the women's movement to shift relationship dynamics with abusive partners.

Awareness of the Origins of Change   Once the women became aware that something about themselves had changed dramatically they began to wonder why. In this stage, the women began to make the connections between the very subtle but widespread changes that had occurred and the behaviour of their partners. Again, it must be noted that this was not an obvious, straightforward process. If a woman's confidence at work was suffering, it might not have been directly clear that the constant harassment of a partner at home was at the root of the problem. Women sifted through a number of reasons for why a particular change had taken place before they saw its connection to the behaviour of their partners. What was required to become aware of the connections was any circumstance in which women attained a more objective, panoramic view of the abuse they were experiencing. Once women were searching for a reason as to why they might have changed and were given the opportunity to place into perspective the behaviour of their partners, then they began to unravel the links between the two. This was not always possible because, as mentioned previously, most women were denied the time and peace of mind to explore this possibility themselves, and many were cut off from friends, family or anyone who might give them a perspective on the abuse they experienced and its impact. First, although women spoke of a general isolation from contact with others, many described one person in their life with whom they could confide to some degree. Relative to the extreme isolation they experienced this single contact was immensely important. Thus although in general women felt cut off from the support of friends and family, a single supportive friend, family member or therapist took on a significant role in women's growing awareness.

Moreover, for those women who did not have contacts outside their relationships, this second type of awareness was minimal when they were in relationships with abusers. They used the degree to which they held the first type of awareness as a resource to progress through the second turn of the spiral. Thus it is not necessary to gain this second type in order to shift the dynamics of control, but, as we will see, the greater the awareness, the greater are the resources upon which women may draw to regain control.

One-fifth of the women (half from the US and half from the UK) found that friends or family aided their process of awareness, and one-sixth of the group (all US) found that therapists provided a helpful perspective. For example, one woman explained how, despite the loss of most friends and the accompanying sense of intense isolation, one friend in particular continued to maintain close contact. She planned meetings with this woman nearly every day, away from.the apartment she shared with her abuser. Most of their meetings were spent with the friend simply listening to the woman, although, at times, she would make pertinent comments on how an event might be related to specific feelings voiced by the woman. Over time, the woman began to trust this friend and, together, they explored her relationship and its impact. Another woman went to see a therapist in the hope of ending the physical abuse that was occurring in the relationship. Again, the support and respect for this woman's experiences displayed by the therapist, and the opportunity to explore how specific events were related to the feelings of the woman, allowed them to uncover together the nature of the emotional impact her partner's behaviour was having upon her. In this way, some women gained the opportunity to explore a different perspective about their relationships in terms of the personal change they had identified.

A second way in which women changed their perspectives and thus awareness about their partners' behaviour and personal change was through observing the impact of abuse on their children. Although they felt it was difficult to see the origins of change within themselves, the opportunity to observe how another person responded to similar circumstances shed light on the issue. Moreover, because the women with children cared deeply about their welfare, realizing that their children were distressed contributed to their motivation to seek its cause. Two-thirds of the women were mothers. They all expressed concern over the impact of abuse on their children. For three of these women, the effect of abuse on children was so apparent that it provided a impetus for thinking about the circumstances in which they lived. These women sensed their children's fear and began to examine more closely the kinds of changes that were occurring in their own lives and the lives of their children. For example, one woman explained:

> I didn't realize what was going on. I really don't think I did. I just thought it was normal for an awful long time. I think one of the things that made me start to realize what was goin' on was when he started to do it to my daughter as well – bullyin'. And I realized she was really frightened of him. Because she just felt this threat of imminent violence as well, all the time. And her school work was sufferin'. She was like a bag of nerves. And I just started to think 'What the hell's goin' on?!'

For this woman, then, the key to recognizing the significance of her partner's behaviour was that she could see clearly how her daughter was responding to bullying similar to that enacted by her partner against herself. The opportunity to observe the impact of his behaviour on someone else allowed her to see how deeply such behaviour could colour and affect her daughter's whole life.

Awareness and Control So, once a woman becomes aware, either of how she and/or her children have changed or of the relationship between these changes and the abuse she experiences, how does this affect the dynamics of power and control within the relationship? First, as women began to gain either type of awareness, they were building a base of knowledge about themselves and/or their relationships. In order to see that they had changed, they must have recognized that, at one time, they were different – more confident, self-accepting, or positive about themselves and life. This knowledge that they had the capacity to be different, and to feel differently about themselves, in itself was a resource upon which to draw when their partners tried to exercise control. For example, just remembering that she was successful in school helped one woman deflect the impact of an abuser's assertion that she was stupid. Knowledge about self, then, was a personal resource which contributed to women's relative power within the relationship.

Secondly, the process of growing awareness focused the women's attention back on themselves and how they had changed. As explained in the description of the inward phase, control was executed through the focusing of women's attention and behaviour on the needs and wishes of the abuser. When women began to attend to themselves they regained contact with many of the personal resources that had been denied to them. Access to the resource of awareness, then, marks another step of outward movement in the spiral, an increase in power which eventually enables women to free themselves from the web of abuse. Thus, awareness can lead to a second factor underlying outward movement, described below.

Reclaiming Power and Leaving an Abuser
In becoming aware of the changes in themselves and, in some cases, the reasons for these changes, women sometimes felt a surge of emotion about what was occurring. Predominantly, women described feeling anger or fear. These emotions were resources upon which the women interviewed drew most heavily in order to move a greater distance outward on the spiral and, ultimately, break free from abuse. Both provided sources of energy which fired women's action for change. I will first discuss the nature of each of these sources of energy and then turn to how, specifically, women used them to regain power and control within their relationships which enabled them to leave their partners.

However, first I must stress that increased awareness may not always lead directly to a surge of emotions. Women may move inward and outward along the spiral for long periods unless they generate a source of energy that supports active change. For example, for many women, awareness fed back into negative self-worth. Because women came to believe that they were worth very little and were unsure of their identity, they associated the changes they had identified in themselves with personal inadequacy. Some women thought that they felt suicidal because they were worthless or that their newly identified negative self-concept was a reflection of their real selves rather than a reaction to the circumstances in which they lived. In this way, awareness of personal change may feed into inward movement and increased abuser control.

There are two forces which may motivate this outward movement towards leaving an abuser. Women may develop anger at the way in which their partner behaves, or may acknowledge feelings of fear, and generate a desire for self-preservation in reaction to this fear, in response to the deep emotional and physical pain that is wrought by abuse. This is the movement along the spiral within the relationship which shifts the power dynamics to the extent that women become able to leave their abusers.

Women's Experiences of Anger   A dimension of anger that was described by the women was its sudden, intense surge of energy which fired them to end their relationships. In this sense, anger was a resource, an energy for change. For just over one-half of the women, their experience of a surge of anger backed attempts to end their relationships with abusers. However, because the intensity of their anger was extreme, the ways in which women contemplated ending their relationships involved immediate action. As a result, whether or not the women perceived opportunities for leaving their partners played an important role in whether use of anger was constructive or destructive to the women.

In terms of using anger constructively, one-tenth of the group left their partners immediately upon experiencing their rage. For these women, the way to leave was apparent, and rage simply clarified their perspectives. For example, one woman was institutionalized by her abuser after she had been drugged to the degree that she could not protest on her own behalf. The sense of utter lack of control over her institutionalization touched in her a deep anger. She described a sense of overwhelming rage towards her partner because she suddenly recognized how damaging his abuse could be – both to her emotional state and to her control over her life. This surge of anger motivated her to end the relationship once and for all. Because she had the financial resources to achieve this, and contact with one friend who was willing to help her, she was able to vanish from her partner's life immediately. Thus rage can motivate women to leave their relationships and deny a partner the opportunity to enact further abuse.

However, the use of anger was not always so straightforward. When women did not perceive or did not have access to opportunities for leaving their partners, anger often emerged unexpectedly. For these women, because they saw no way of escaping the relationship, their anger remained unacknowledged until it reached a level at which it could no longer be ignored. They described feeling blasts of powerful rage which seemed to come out of the blue and emerged in dreams or in interactions with the abusers which did not appear to be abusive. Because these women saw no way to leave their partners immediately, this sudden anger fired them to consider drastic ways of ending their relationships. For nearly half of the women, anger backed serious consideration of ending relationships through murder or suicide.

Contemplation of killing their abusers was one of the channels for expression of the anger and self-preservation that began to emerge:

> He had beat me up yet again and I threw a plate at him and I got a knife and held him in a corner and I said to him: 'I'm going to kill you' . . . and I knew, my mind was racing, I thought I'm so angry I know I can kill him. I was really going to kill him. And I had gotten to a place where I wasn't just like 'I'm gonna kill you,' I wanted to feel his blood. I wanted to put that blade in his back and just go straight down. I could see it. I could feel it.

The sense of rage expressed by these women demonstrates the depth of anger felt by abused women in this research. The only way of changing their circumstances, and acting on the energy of rage, in their eyes at that moment, was to kill their partners.[6] Yet, as I will discuss later, when the depth of this anger was expressed to an abuser, although the wish to kill was not fulfilled, women significantly shifted the imbalance of power in their relationships. In this way, anger which was focused on a highly destructive aim communicated both to women and their abusers that they held a resource upon which they might draw to protest the power and control maintained over them.

Similarly, other women spoke of self-destruction as the only avenue for change. For these women, there did not exist safe circumstances in which they were able to allow their anger to emerge or be expressed. For example, for some, their abusers' violence was so extreme that they feared any challenge to his or her behaviour might spark a life-threatening attack. Or, for other women, simply feeling trapped in the relationship convinced them that expression of anger would be useless. As a result, anger turned into suicidal thoughts. The women described how suicidal feelings were closely linked to an urge to kill an abuser. Two women's comments express this link between their urges to kill their partners and to kill themselves:

> I really thought – there were several times when he beat me up really badly and made me have sex with him and then passed out. And I thought about killing him. But I knew that it wouldn't work. I knew that he would kill me . . . So then I would go contemplate killing myself because those seemed to be the only two choices.

> And the other thing was that I also realized that the thought of killing me or killing her seemed like options. I mean I never decided to, but they were ideas I seriously considered.

These women describe how the desire to be safe from abuse at whatever cost – a desire rooted in anger – can manifest itself as a desire to commit suicide because the options for change seem so limited. Thus, in addition to the loss of hope described as inward movement along the spiral which contributes to suicidal thoughts, the lack of opportunity to express anger may also contribute to the depowering and destructive experiences described by women.

Moreover, feminist therapists have identified how women, in general, have difficulty in identifying and expressing their anger, because of their gender-linked socialization (Lerner, 1990; Eichenbaum and Orbach, 1985). In accordance with this, women described extreme difficulty in recognizing and acknowledging the full strength of their anger towards their abusers. The fact that this anger, for many of them, was an essential tool in breaking free from abuse, and that the culture in which they live promotes the loss of this tool in women, indicates another way in which abuse and the dynamics of control are linked to and supported by the social construction of masculinity and femininity.

Fear and Self-Preservation   A second source of energy upon which women draw to end their relationships is the dimension of fear,[7] which energizes action for self-preservation. Self-preservation, for the women interviewed, was a basic gut reaction rooted in fear – fear that if circumstances continued as they were, some sort of serious and irreparable damage would occur. Such circumstances may be as immediate as a violent attack, or may be more diffusely experienced as women begin to recognize the long-term emotional damage they are suffering. Like anger, it is generally experienced by women as an overwhelming sensation, a desperate need to make change. From the interviews, two ways emerged in which fear and self-preservation played a role in changing the power dynamics.

First, self-preservation was experienced by some women as a confusing sense that something needed to change. Women often described how they were unsure of what to change but they knew that they had to act. They were responding at the first type of awareness – knowing that they had changed in negative ways – and yet were unsure of why. With awareness of changes in themselves and without recognition of cause, women felt fear and the need to prevent, in some way, further changes.

For example, one woman's partner enacted his abuse almost entirely through overburdening of responsibility. Within the relationship, as she reported it, it was extremely difficult for her to recognize that her partner's repeated display of childish behaviour and lack of responsibility had encouraged her to become insensitive to her own needs and perspectives and to focus on those of her partner. Consequently, as described in relation to inward movement, she became unsure of her value and ability. She attained the first type of awareness concerning these changes when she became unable to function and found that she could no longer care for their children. Over time, she became suicidal and addicted to tranquillizers. However, at the point at which she nearly took her life she felt a gut response of self-preservation. Her action was focused not on changing her relationship but simply on removing herself from her entire way of life. She rang acquaintances in another city and went to stay with them, explaining that she needed a break. What she actually felt was that she needed to try anything, desperately, to save her life. It was only with the execution of this impulse that she was able to begin to unravel the impact her partner's behaviour was having and, in time, she left the marriage.

The lack of certainty about the origins of impulses for self-preservation of this kind is described in the following quotes:

> I really felt like I was not only losing myself but I didn't even know what that self was. And that I really needed to be by myself to figure that out.

> There was a point where I didn't want anything to do with my children. I'd lost my own identity and sense of what I wanted so much – I didn't want anything that I had already, I just wanted to up and be somewhere else, and be a different person.

Here their assertions that 'I really needed to be by myself', and 'I just wanted to up and be somewhere else', attest to the way in which fear and self-preservation motivate women to make change.

Secondly, women who experienced severe, life-threatening violence acted on fear and the need for self-preservation in response to a specific event. In these cases, women knew exactly what they were attempting to preserve themselves from and why they had to act immediately. One-half of the women felt the need to leave their relationships because of their deep fear that the violence was potentially permanently injurious or fatal to themselves or their children. For example, one woman left her house immediately upon finding that her partner had attempted to rape her daughter. She was suddenly overpowered by fear for her daughter in response to this drastic form of abuse. She phoned a friend, packed as much as she could hold, and rushed across town in panic. Another woman was being beaten and told by her abuser that he was going to kill her, as her quote in the previous chapter attests. Although the house was locked she used her deep desire to save her life in outrunning her partner and escaping through the one door that she correctly guessed he might have left open. Thus there are two ways in which women experience self-preservation: as a confusing urge to change some aspect of their lives, and as an immediate response to an event which threatens their and/or their children's lives or safety.

The Role of Anger and Fear in Leaving an Abuser   In taking immediate action towards leaving partners, as described in the sections above, the women clearly achieved a major shift in the power dynamics, marking the final outward movement in the spiral. First, they denied their partners the opportunity to assert further control over them. Secondly, they created and drew upon many resources in order to reassert their own control. In this second aspect of the shift, women actually discovered or created for themselves resources upon which to draw. The erosion of their relationships with friends and family, for example, was overcome by recontacting those people with whom they had had little contact, revealing their circumstances and asking for specific support such as transport, money or accommodation. This process entailed a significant factor of risk. Women were required to reveal aspects of their lives which they had hidden and felt embarrassed about. However, in doing so, they were able to ask for the support which had not been offered previously, and, in some cases, this support was granted. Moreover, the women used their own creativity in finding ways to support their actions. For example, one woman asked her friend to drive her to the place where her partner was living and stole his expensive sports car, which afforded her transportation over the first few months of separation. Anger and self-preservation, in these cases, fuelled the action taken and motivated women to create and draw upon the external resources around them and secure a way of leaving.

For the other two-thirds of the group, for whom leaving was not an immediately recognized solution to shifting the power imbalance, the use of anger and self-preservation actually worked to temporarily shift the control within the relationship, allowing them a period in which to begin to contemplate the act. The ways in which this was achieved differ somewhat depending on whether women were driven predominantly by anger or by self-preservation. Hence, I will address each in turn, and then look at how such a delicate process of asserting power within the relationship, in the long run, can lead to leaving a partner.

Anger worked in two ways to temporarily shift the imbalance of power and control within relationships described by women. As discussed above, anger was experienced as intense surges of energy. Even when this energy was not used to end the relationship completely, its expression had significant impact on the control and power women regained and, ultimately, their ability to leave an abuser. First, the expression of anger, whether in thought or action, significantly altered the power dynamics of the relationship. Anger was the expression of self and self-worth that the women lost as they moved inward on the spiral. It was a statement that women felt they did not deserve abuse and would act to stop the abuse. It was a deep reclaiming of self on an emotional level. When this occurred, the damage of emotional abuse began to lessen and the effects of further emotional abuse ceased to feed into the cycle of decreased control.

Second, anger also signalled change to abusers, that the women did possess a powerful resource upon which they may draw to combat the control their partners exerted. No women found that their anger actually changed the behaviour of their partners to the extent that they stopped their abusive behaviour. Because of this, anger as an assertion of power was ultimately a key to leaving rather than changing the relationship. Yet, the deep and real intensity of their hate and their determination to protect themselves was expressed in a way that could not be ignored by their abusers, and this affirmation contributed to women's sense of their own power. For example, a woman who dreamt of violence described her dream in a joint counselling session with her partner:

> I did have this dream and I used to grab him by the balls until I got him on the floor, and I'd always be wearing high heeled shoes which I never wear, and I'd stamp and stamp on his face until his nose was flat to his face.

She described her partner's reaction as one of shock and fear, as if he had no thought that she might retaliate in response to the abuse he had perpetrated. This reaction confirmed to her that she did have potential resources which might afford her power, because her anger was potent enough to frighten the man who had been, up to this point, largely in control of her life. Other women described threatening to kill their abusers when they attacked. For example, one woman drove off her abuser by wielding a knife and letting him know, in no uncertain terms, that she would use the weapon against him if he continued his attack. Her threats backed up with sincere and vivid rage signalled to her partner that she was determined to protect herself at all costs. In these instances, when women caught their abusers off guard, they began to understand that they did have power in the relationship, that their abusers were not all powerful. The abuser may not have changed his or her behaviour in response to anger. In fact, it is essential to recognize that any expression of anger to an abusive partner always carries the risk that the partner will escalate his or her violence or emotional assaults in an attempt to regain the control that a woman's anger threatens. Anger was most safely recognized and expressed when coupled with the self-protective energy of fear. However, anger may give women a glimmer of their own personal power, and move them to begin recognizing the energetic resources they hold to enable them to leave their abusers.

As with anger, the energy for self-preservation which accompanies fear was a resource which shifted the power imbalance of the relationships and eventually, if not immediately, allowed the women interviewed to regain sufficient control over their lives to leave their relationships. Like the women who decided to leave immediately upon experiencing fear, these women created resources upon which they could draw. They sought therapists, began to bridge the lack of communication with friends or left for a temporary period in order to think things out regarding the relationship. Although they felt that their partners might be angry at their actions, their drive overcame that concern, and if they felt it necessary, they acted in secrecy in order to protect themselves. In this way, their fear and desire for self-preservation served to overturn some of the mechanisms of control used by their abusers. These women began to receive information from friends or therapists or gained time to pay attention to their own needs and wishes. In doing so, they regained resources which had been denied them by their partners and thus altered the power imbalance. As this imbalance began to shift, they gained more power and control with which to create the opportunity to leave their relationships. Thus, two thirds of the women organized themselves with regard to gaining access to mutually held funds and taking with them any necessary documents or possessions. Some women began to save what little income they were allotted over long periods, such as years, until they felt they had accumulated enough to leave. Others began to search the papers for private accommodation, work out whether they could survive on the income they earned from their jobs, and actually take steps to securing rented accommodation. For these women, their plans were much more thought out and gradual than were those who acted immediately on the energy associated with anger or fear. They used the gradual building of self-preservation or the periodic surges of anger to energize each step of their plan to leave.

For both women who left immediately in response to a specific event and those who planned their leaving over a period of months to years, the first time they left may not have been the last. As recorded in much of the literature on battered women, women may return a number of times to their partners because of either practical or emotional ties (Bowker, 1983; Dobash and Dobash, 1980; NiCarthy, 1986; Pahl, 1985b). The women in this group were no different. Just under one-third returned at least once to live with their abusers. However, in terms of gaining resources, every experience of leaving added to women's knowledge about living independently and about the fact that it was possible for them to leave. Leaving and returning, then, were part of a gaining of power in relation to an abuser for the women interviewed. They were building their personal resources of knowledge which, in time, allowed them to leave their partners forever, although, for some, this took years to achieve. Women who returned had not failed to shift the power imbalance. They were simply still in the process of regaining their own power and control and shifting the degree of control their partners had over them.

In the experience of the women interviewed, the choice of leaving was the only option which would ensure that they could maintain the control over their lives gained from their progression through the spiral. Women thought that, although their recognition of change and anger afforded them greater power and control within their relationships, this challenged their abusers' control but did not shift the fundamental behaviour and desire they saw in their abusers to regain and hold greater control. In other words, a shift in the balance of power allowed women to break free from the abuse but did not lead to the equality of power which would allow women to remain in their relationships without being abused.

Dynamics of Control and the Web of Emotional Abuse

In conclusion, the dynamics of power and control which were conceptualized as a spiral become even more clear when seen in the context of the web of abuse. When women are experiencing their partners as holding more power and exerting greater control over their lives, they move inward along the spiral towards the centre of the web. The spaces between the binding strands of web become smaller; there is increasingly greater contact with the many different web strands as they converge. Thus a woman moving inward becomes more powerless to escape. Every move she makes is likely to put her in contact with another strand, binding her more firmly to the web. As she moves outward on her path, the space between strands increases. She gains more freedom to move, to see beyond the web, to encounter avenues of possible escape. At the edges of the spiral, the web is more open space than it is sticky strands, affording a woman more freedom to use her energy for escape rather than holding her more strongly with every move she makes.

It is no coincidence that this imagery of slowly struggling through a web which has been constructed to bind a woman is frightening and seemingly perilous. It is true that, just as a fly caught in a spider's web may be fatally attacked at any moment, regardless of how close they are to escaping, an abused woman may be killed or permanently injured, or may commit suicide or homicide as a result of the abuse. According to women's stories, danger was always an element of their experiences as long as they were in relationships with their abusers, and even sometimes after they had left, and regardless of their direction of movement on the spiral. Thus the imagery of a web is complete. It both describes the interrelation of the components of abuse and the dynamics of power, and symbolizes the immensity and intensity of the danger experienced throughout their relationships by the women interviewed.

In addition, it is important to note that the concept of a spiral which describes the dynamics of power and control does not cover all the issues the women faced in leaving abusive partners. There were many social and practical circumstances which further served as obstacles to leaving. Although this chapter focuses on the power dynamics within the relationship, it is not meant to suggest that this is the sole obstacle women face. As the above descriptions of how women left attest, material and social obstacles such as finding housing, support and funding are all part of the problems women had to overcome. As the following chapter demonstrates, shifting the power dynamics and leaving a partner were only the first step in grappling with these problems.

Notes

1 As in my analysis, sociological debate about the concept of control is closely linked to that about the concept of power (see below). My use of the term is defined in the text. However, other sociologists have pointed out that, as a general term, its definition is contestable (Gibbs, 1989).

2 Sociologists have debated about the definition of 'power' (Etzioni, 1968; Gibbs, 1989; Hawley, 1963; Lukes, 1976; Martin, 1977; Olsen, 1970), as it is used in a wide spectrum of analyses which range from the level of individual human interaction to that of social organization and politics. Fundamentally, all definitions hinge on the idea that one person or group has an effect on another person or group. This notion is also central to my approach in that I am defining power in terms of the degree of influence an abuser has over an abused woman relative to the amount of influence she has over her own life. Although my analysis does not enter into the debate over the definition of power, as my use of the term reflects a central aspect of the interviews and does not define power, it does reflect the essence of the underlying definitions forwarded within this debate.

3 Campbell (1984) discusses a diversity of psychological definitions for self-esteem which include a force underlying human motivation and desire to succeed (James, 1910; Kaplan, 1975), the degree to which a person's ideal and actual concepts of self correspond (Cohen, 1968), and 'an awareness of possession of desirable qualities or objects by oneself' (Campbell, 1984: 7). My use of the term is similar to Campbell's in that it reflects women's sense of self-respect and self-regard, rather than a psychological approach to understanding human motivation.

4 Identity, in terms of this analysis, relates closely to the notion of 'self' expressed by women. Identity is the conscious recognition of the elements and perspectives that contribute to a sense of self. Again, the use of this term in such an unproblematic way is intended to reflect the women's use and perceptions, although other literature has addressed the debate about defining identity and its relation to 'self' (Bruner et al., 1956; Blumer, 1969; Foote, 1951; McCall and Simmons, 1966; Strauss, 1959). McCall and Simmons (1966), for example, argue that identity and identification are fundamentally a process in which people categorize and symbolize human interaction.

5 Psychological research has used the term 'depression' to refer to many types of psychological states (Friedman, 1974; Gilbert, 1984; Mendels, 1970; Rowe, 1978). Friedman (1974) identified three ways in which it is used: to describe an affect, a clinical state, and a character style. However, I use the term to refer to affect, a feeling of sadness or loss (Friedman, 1974). Specifically, women experienced a feeling of depression in response to a loss of hope.

6 Browne has explored the experiences of women who have felt so trapped that they acted on this rage and actually murdered their abusers, attesting to the desperation and depth of anger experienced (Browne, 1987). Radford and Kelly (1991) conceptualize murder committed by abused women as 'self-preservation' in advocating for legal reform. However, in the group interviewed, none actually attempted suicide or killing their partners, although, at times, some seriously considered these options.

7 Fear has been identified in Chapter 3 as a component of emotional abuse because the emotional and physical damage that accompanies experiencing it over long periods impairs women's lives and is painful and traumatic to them. However, another dimension of fear is the energy which accompanies it and can be used for self-preservation. This is the dimension of fear addressed in this chapter and is distinct from its painful and traumatic characteristics discussed in Chapter 3.

5

Obstacles to Securing Independence

Thus far I have addressed the emotional impact of abuse and leaving an abuser from the perspective of women. However, women also spoke at length about the variety and importance of the issues they confronted which were external to their subjective feelings. This chapter addresses women's emphases on how their daily lives centred around resolving matters such as setting up an independent life, particularly in the first year after their relationships had ended, and the impact of the dramatic change.

Hoff, Marin and Pahl interviewed women within their first year after leaving an abusive partner and found, like this research, that practical needs are foremost in women's concerns (Hoff, 1990; Marin, 1985; Pahl, 1985b).[1] This study also provides information about women's experiences *after* the first year and about the experiences of women who do not use shelters or refuges.[2]

In general, women spoke of four major categories of basic needs: obtaining housing; financial support; medical advice or attention; and physical and emotional safety. This section identifies the practical needs of the women interviewed, discusses how they went about getting these met, and provides insight into the effectiveness of institutional and organizational responses to women's needs.

The First Steps to an Independent Life: Finding Housing and Economic Resources

By far the most prominent problem facing women once they have left their abusers is finding adequate housing and sufficient income to survive. These two aspects of their needs are often confronted at the same time, immediately after leaving an abuser, and are interrelated in that securing accommodation can absorb a major portion of a woman's limited financial resources. Fundamental to resolving these issues is attaining information and knowledge about the resources and aid available, and thus this topic will be discussed first.

All the British women and three-quarters of the US women experienced problems in attaining finances or housing and/or lack of knowledge about attaining finances or housing. Only one-tenth of the women, then, did not feel that these issues were significant. This was because they did not live with their abusers during their relationships and they were already employed at the time the relationship ended. However, for the rest, housing, finances and lack of knowledge were cited as major contributing factors in their feelings of stress and were identified as obstacles to the success of their attempts to leave their partners and establish security. The material obstacles addressed here are extremely significant to women not only because finances and housing are required for physical survival, but also because they are related to women's emotional need for safety in order to cope with the tremendous impact of abuse described in Chapter 6.

The Context of Attaining Material Independence: a Dearth of Knowledge

The process of attaining finances and housing is begun with knowing what to do. Women were often faced with an entirely new situation: some had never applied for government aid, did not know if they were eligible, and had little knowledge about what types of aid were available; some did not know how to go about seeking employment and finding private accommodation, or even what questions to ask or where to go to find out the answers.

It was clear from the women in this study that such knowledge was not readily available. There were few comprehensive information networks, in either the US or the UK, into which they could tap. Usually when women described to one institution their current situation, it would act on one aspect of this but would not refer them to all the other agencies which might be able to help. The following quote typifies the kinds of frustrating run-arounds women confronted in finding safety for themselves and their children:

> But what I found difficult, well more than difficult, was the fact that you think you're going to get some sense from some social worker who's going to say something to you. I mean what I wanted was an answer and what I got was the arms up, I mean you don't get an answer, you just do not get an answer, you'll get somebody who'll sit and listen to you who won't say anything back to you hardly.

Thus, even though she had access to a service agency, she found that the representative was unable to provide her with the practical information she needed. When, eventually, she tracked down an agency which was more able to address her problems, she found that they were not as unsolvable as her social worker had suggested. She managed to gain information about the specific options open to her and how to go about exercising them.

The only exception to this lack of information networks was exhibited in women's experiences of refuges and a particular agency aiding single parents. One-third of the group (half from the US and half from Britain) had contact with these specific agencies which provided the appropriate help and information women needed to significantly ease the problems of finding housing and finances.

For the two-thirds who did not gain access to such a network, however, lack of information contributed to the stress they felt. One woman, who left her partner within three years before the interview, expressed a typical reaction of distress in response to her lack of knowledge, and described how deeply lack of knowledge affected her experience:

> I thought, I don't know what to do, what benefits to go to or anything. I just didn't know. I was frightened that I'd end up, just, completely lost. I just didn't know what to do.

Not only, then, did women suffer because lack of knowledge complicated their processes of securing housing and finances, but they also suffered because this lack compounded their feelings of fear and vulnerability discussed in the previous chapter. Only once information was uncovered could women begin to confront the actual processes of obtaining housing and finances and building a materially secure life. The details of these processes are described in the following three sections.

Housing: Short-Term Solutions

If a woman has been living with her abuser, as nine-tenths of the women in this group had, then separation requires that she must either remove the abuser from their home or leave the home herself. As she has found negotiating living with her abuser impossible, it is risky and may be dangerous for her to force her abuser to leave. In addition, if a woman fears for her physical safety then she must avoid confrontation with her abuser when she leaves, as did one-half of the women I interviewed. At the point of leaving, when women take final action to free themselves from their partners' control, the risk for escalated retaliation is greatest (Walker, 1979a). Thus she must leave her home, possibly with children, quickly and secretly, and often with few possessions. At this point, whether the separation is accomplished on her own, or with the support of family and friends, or even without intervention from her abuser, the woman is faced with an immediate need for housing and the finances required to move into a new home. The women interviewed described a number of short-term and long-term solutions, none of which are without associated problems. This section describes the short-term solutions, and the next section the long-term solutions.

Many women needed temporary, short-term housing solutions, either because it was impossible to immediately arrange permanent housing or because they were not prepared to face the demands of attaining permanent housing. If problems with long-term housing were extreme, this 'choice' was the only solution other than homelessness. Short-term solutions include staying with friends and family or at refuges. Which of these two solutions occurred depended on the amount of protection and secrecy a woman needed to be safe from her abuser, whether or not she was aware of and felt her circumstances warranted help from refuges, her relations with her friends and family, and the amount of help these parties were willing to offer. Thus even temporary solutions were complex and sometimes problematic.

Just over one-third of the group interviewed stayed with family or friends for a period of a few months to a year. For some women this temporary solution was extremely beneficial as they gained emotional support from the people with whom they stayed. One woman, for example, expressed that the continual support from friends prevented her from ending her pain with suicide. For others, however, these temporary living conditions were more problematic and added to the sense of distress they already were experiencing. For example, one woman lived in crowded conditions with her sister. In these circumstances, she felt that she was under pressure to conform to the living style of her sister's family and that her experience of abuse was of little concern to her sister who had a tremendous amount of her own worries in bringing up a family on a low income. As a result, her living conditions compounded the intense emotions she experienced, rather than relieved them. Thus, with the emotional stress that accompanies leaving an abuser, the support or lack thereof they received from those they lived with comprised a major factor in whether this short-term solution was seen to be beneficial.

In contrast to women who stayed temporarily with friends or family, one-fifth of the British and one-fourth of the US women resided in refuges immediately after leaving their abusers.[3] Refuges for battered women, which are free or available at low cost, can play an important role in women's early experiences of leaving abusers. In both Britain and the US refuges generally form a network in which, if the one contacted is not able to accommodate an abused woman, the workers there will refer her to or contact other refuges that have available space. There is evidence, however, that the lack of funding for refuges which meet the needs of racially oppressed women forces women of colour who utilize this network to confront issues of racism in addition to the trauma they have incurred from abuse. Although refuges were seen to be extremely useful to the women interviewed, the lack of racially and culturally relevant services persists as a problem (Mama, 1989a).

British refuges offered the women who used them accommodation until they had permanent housing. This meant that, as council housing often had a waiting list of over a year, the British women generally resided in refuges for up to or over a year. This period allowed them to wait for council housing without being identified as 'voluntarily homeless', to find appropriate private housing, or to wait for a period of relative safety in which they could move back into their old homes. Conversely, US refuges required that women stayed no longer than six weeks, unless they had been active in seeking but unable to attain housing within this time. As a result, the US women interviewed were not able to attain state provided housing because, as in Britain, the waiting list is extremely long. Instead, US women were aided in searching for low cost housing and in obtaining state funding.

The benefits of refuge residence were gained along with the stress of living in often overcrowded accommodation for an unpredictable time. Despite the differences between US and British services, this was an issue for all the women who had lived in refuges and has been noted by others to be a problem for formerly abused women (Hoff, 1990; Marin, 1985; Pahl, 1978; 1985b). Both US and British services are over-crowded and overwhelming from the perspective of women who have used them. Lack of privacy, resident conflict, and imposition of refuge rules added to women's sense of confusion and trauma.[4] Because women often share rooms and facilities with others whom they don't know and who may come from a race, culture or class with which they have little experience, there is tension and conflict. For example, one woman described how she was used to putting her children to bed quite late relative to the other residents. The other residents felt angry that these children were awake when they wanted peaceful, adult con-versation during the evening. Such conflicts in lifestyle lead to tension and resentment amongst residents. For British women who reside in refuges for up to a year, the stress of these conditions is extreme. The period is often too long to cope with such crowded conditions, and the women interviewed spoke of feeling disheartened as their coresidents returned to their homes with their abusers rather than continuing to live at the refuge and wait for housing.

Despite this, all the women who resided at shelters or refuges regarded the help they received as invaluable and expressed deep gratitude that such aid was available to them. In addition to a roof over their heads, women benefited from the knowledge that refuge workers held about state institutions and how to apply for aid. They also felt that they were able to express their feelings in an environment where staff respected them, and other residents shared similar experiences, whether or not they had access to regular and formal counselling. This allowed them the kind of support they needed to feel affirmed and valued.

Housing: Long-Term Solutions
Regardless of the quality of short-term accommodation, ultimately women face the problem of finding appropriate long-term housing. They can either negotiate with their partners over formerly shared housing or seek other accommodation. For safety reasons, most of the women interviewed chose the latter route. The following sections will discuss the problems and benefits associated with these solutions.

Negotiating over Previously Shared Housing   Just over one-fifth of the women chose to negotiate with their abusive partners for sole access to previously shared housing or half of the value of owned property. Although, on the one hand, this alleviated some of the practical issues of finding new houses and minimized the amount of injustice expressed by the women about having to move from or lose their own homes through no fault of their own, it also presented obvious problems.

First, in negotiating over an owned home, as did two women in this study (one US, one British), legal processes were drawn out and became a milieu for the abuse enacted by their partners. One of the women related:

> She was intractable . . . we're talkin' every square inch of this deal we had to walk over and she, every single step of the way, screaming that she was getting ripped off by me, that I was so cold.

Over a period of a few months this woman was recommended by her lawyers to move back into the house with her abuser in order to reinforce her status as an owner in the eyes of the court. During this period she suffered from intense verbal and emotional abuse. Even when such attempts are successful, the process can provide an avenue by which the ex-partner can continue to enact abuse.

Another problem in negotiating over shared housing was removing the abusers from the property. If women overcome the financial problems, discussed later, in taking over full rent or mortgage of a home, then this is an option. One-sixth of the group remained in their old homes and confronted the issue of being safe while living in a location known by their abusers. In the section on protection which follows, the solutions generated by women are discussed. In these cases, women carefully gauged whether and what kind of external intervention would sufficiently impress their ex-partners to inhibit their abuse. Thus, for some, backing from courts which decreed that a woman had the right to the shared home, and that the abuser must not enter it, was sufficient to keep a partner from continuing to harass the woman. For others, court rulings had to be backed up by the police or friends and family who were willing to protect formerly abused women.

A final problem with negotiating for previously shared housing is that, when women opt to live in the homes where abuse occurred, they are constantly reminded by association with their surroundings of painful memories of assaults or feelings about abuse. Women struggled to overcome this by redecorating and rearranging their homes, although on a low income this kind of reclaiming of their homes was difficult.

On the whole, women expressed a preference for finding private accommodation when possible for two reasons. Private accommodation, rented or owned, signified a status of independence and self-sufficiency. Because women had been abused by the people they most trusted, this independence and self-sufficiency seemed highly attractive. Secondly, attaining private accommodation relieved women from interacting with state housing institutions which, as will be discussed, can be highly problematic, stressful and dehumanizing.

Finding New Housing One major difference between the US and British women was the degree to which they were able to secure private or public accommodation. US women tended to have more opportunity and more material resources to acquire private accommodation, whereas British women had more access to state housing and extended temporary accommodation which enabled them to wait to be offered state housing. Thus, three-quarters of the US women and one-tenth of the British women eventually found permanent housing in privately rented accommodation. In contrast, nearly one-half of the British women and no US women sought to be relocated in state housing. Yet, whether women used state financial aid to fund living in private housing, had sufficient private funds to afford private housing or relied on state housing, they faced obstacles in doing so. Some of the most commonly addressed problems were as follows.

Women using state financial aid to fund private accommodation faced finding scarce, inexpensive but adequate housing. This was particularly difficult for women with children. Women told of daily searching the papers, often finding no accommodation which would meet their needs and would be affordable. When they did manage to find accommodation at a low rent, it was frequently too small for their families, or in areas of the city which they felt were dangerous. Moreover, women with low incomes or on state financial aid found that their ability to pay rent was questioned by landlords. Thus they were often turned away from the few locations they had found which were appropriate to their needs.

Even women who had adequate finances to pay for private housing faced problems. For many women, because of the financial control exerted by their former abusers, the costs of independent living are unknown. They are frightened that each month they will not be able to pay the bills and may feel it necessary to live extremely frugally until they are convinced of their capacity to manage their finances. Fear of the unknown, in some cases reinforced by messages from their abuser that they cannot manage money, compounds the trauma of finding a new home and establishing independence.

Finally, the benefits in seeking council or state housing are simply that adequate housing can be attained at an affordable price. However, women who accepted this route did so only as a last option. For these women, negotiations with the housing departments were often frustrating and humiliating and thus played a major role in the amount of stress and frustration they experienced. For example, three British women found that the council did not accept their requests for housing because, in the state's eyes, their temporary residence with family or friends exempted them from being defined as 'homeless'. This status of 'voluntary homelessness' placed these women low on the council's list of priorities. Consequently, these women felt that they had to contribute a considerable amount of time and energy towards convincing the council that they were in need of housing. This entailed describing their private and painful experiences of abuse in detail for the judgement of officials who may or may not believe them. In some cases, women were forced to the denigrating position of desperately pleading with a council official for consideration. Considering what they have already suffered, the pain of such experiences is particularly acute for formerly abused women. Despite the violence and abuse which drove them from their home, creative solutions for temporary housing, and the reality that such solutions could not be permanent, women found it difficult and traumatic to gain priority on the housing waiting list.

Moreover, once offered housing, they had to negotiate for appropriate terms. One woman described being offered small, dirty, soon to be demolished flats for herself and three children. Another was forced to live at a bed and breakfast with her children until more appropriate housing could be found. Her experience underscores the desperation felt by women caught within the state housing system. At the time of interview she expressed her wish that she had stayed with her abusive partner. She is the only woman of the group interviewed who thought this, and she attributed it entirely to her experience in attempting to attain housing and finances from the state institutions:

> So I just got out as fast as I could. Which is the biggest mistake of my life, to get out. Cause when I came back [here] as a single parent, they just didn't want to know ya. 'Why did you leave your home, you had everything?' I said 'Because he was so violent.' I did have bruises and things to prove that he'd hit me and the local council just took no notice. I've been in bed and

breakfast 15 weeks now, in one room with three children, no cooking facilities, I can't even make a drink. Fifteen weeks!

She stressed that abuse from her partner, although increasingly violent and emotional, was preferable to the abuse she received from state institutions.

There are many ways in which women meet their housing needs but all entail their own set of problems and anxieties. The problems associated with both temporary and permanent housing are central issues in the experience of formerly abused women, as is also the impact such problems have on their emotional state.

Finances

There are two issues of significance in the way in which women discussed finances. These are attaining sufficient economic support, and their experiences of financial independence.

Attaining Economic Support   There are a variety of ways in which the women were able to meet their financial needs. Two-thirds of them managed without state financial aid. This required having access to financial resources, such as personal savings, or the opportunity to work and the freedom from using high cost child care. Such resources were more common to the US women interviewed for this research. Half of the US and one of the British women were currently employed at the time they separated from their abuser. Furthermore, one-quarter of the US and one of the British women found an opportunity for employment, and acceptable child care when needed, at the time of separation.

If women did not have the resources or opportunity to support themselves, then they sought state aid. Shelter residence contributed significantly to women's experiences of attaining state financial aid because refuge staff used their authority with state institutions and expertise to negotiate on behalf of the residents. Because of this, US refuge residents experienced little problem with either applying for or being granted state financial support.

Women interviewed who did not have the support of refuge or shelter staff in applying for state aid (three-quarters of the UK women and one US woman) faced abuse similar to that experienced in applying for state housing. State aid workers questioned women's eligibility in a way thought by women to be degrading and humiliating. Like most of them, the woman quoted below told how her experience with gaining state aid was one of the most emotionally and practically arduous obstacles she faced:

> The hardest thing is organizing yourself with the [DSS]. 'Cause they think everyone should be either a wino or a drop out, and you don't get a penny unless you're penniless . . .' They'd look at me clothes, and I make me own clothes so they look respectable, and they say 'Oh, how much did that cost?' They want to know what you're spending your money on . . . if you're makin' it go further, they think 'She doesn't need it' . . . it took ages to convince 'em I was waiting behind my letter box for my giro cheque to buy food.

As with their experiences with state housing, considering that these women have just ended relationships in which their partners may have placed similar economic constraints and demands upon them, and that women typically felt degraded by their ex-partners' abuse, confronting these responses from the DSS can be particularly difficult and painful for formerly abused women.

In addition, women found that the state financial aid agencies encouraged them to accept maintenance from their partners. Although the state agency agreed to collect this maintenance, of the women offered this alternative one-half rejected the idea. They explained that this residual dependence on their partners seemed risky and potentially problematic. These fears were not unfounded. One woman who agreed to allow maintenance to be collected rather than receive full state support met resistance from the DSS one year later:

> Oh my God! I mean there's always something what reminds you. You think everything's going. But then the other week I got a letter from the [DSS] sayin' that maintenance will stop and I have to collect the maintenance now from [my ex husband] and I thought 'Oh my God!'

For this woman and the majority of the others, collecting any sum of money on a regular basis from an ex-partner who was abusive was seen not only as potentially unstable financially, but also as jeopardizing their physical and emotional safety. Their experiences highlight problems with current US and UK policies in which seeking child care and support from absent parents is statutory. Recognition but little practical change, at least in the UK, has been made with regard to the safety of women who leave abusive partners.

Yet, there are exceptions to the usual experience of attaining state aid as problematic. In both the US and the UK, state aid offers a basic sum to applicants, but discretionary payments depend on whether women know about them and feel able to insist that they are paid. For a few, finding access to different discretionary funds made their experience with state aid considerably more beneficial than that of others. One woman found a unique way to secure state benefit which attests to the creativity of formerly battered women in the face of difficult circumstances. She applied to the DSS and obtained their guarantee to pay the interest on a mortgage, leaving her to pay the endowment. After extensive negotiations with mortgage brokers for a 100 per cent mortgage she managed to purchase a house for which she is paying out of her income support. For this woman, seeking assistance from the DSS to support her investment in an owned home seemed to be more fruitful than other women's experiences with applying for council housing. Perhaps because she applied for aid that was different from simply subsistence income, she gained more interest and cooperation from the DSS. Although the purchase required extreme budgeting of other expenses, she was pleased that she was building her financial resources by paying mortgage rather than rent. Thus despite the often degrading attitude taken by state funding institutions, there are unique circumstances in which women may create empowering solutions.

Maintaining Financial Independence   Even once the initial obstacles in securing finances and permanent housing are overcome, women face daily battles in maintaining their independence and, in some cases, such circumstances persist for years after leaving an abuser. Nearly all the British women and one-half of the US women who had dependent children identified financial hardship as one of the major long-term stresses faced after leaving their partners. These women described juggling finances, and continual worry about making funds last through the month. For women who did not have dependent children, the stresses of financial independence were sorted out in the first year to year and a half after the separation. In contrast, women with dependent children described how financial stress played a long-term role in their lives:

> I still don't have any more than I had 20 years ago in terms of material things . . . And I had terrible credit problems . . . there was some state income tax thing that we ended up owing and they came back after it, after like seven years later. And they took all my money . . . and they never went after him because he wasn't in the state . . . He never paid child support, even that time I had to quit because of the taxes . . . he wouldn't even bring food for the kids. It totally affected my life, a lot.

For the one-half of the US women who did not have children, fear of financial problems at the outset of leaving their partners, and the trauma of negotiating a division of property on separation, featured more largely in their accounts than did long-term financial distress. One woman remarked on her fear of the unknown with regard to supporting herself financially:

> [were finances a problem?] Oh yeah . . . well, scary. And I did get stuck with half the credit card bills which was close to $1500. So I didn't know what I could afford. I took a very cheap furnished apartment, I didn't know.[5]

In sum, the financial and housing issues confronting formerly abused women are, in many ways, similar to those experienced by all women who leave their partners. The poverty of women, and the existence of state systems structured to support the needs of two-parent hetero-sexual families, make independence an issue for all women. However, the facts that women are many times fleeing for their lives and emotional well-being, and are often in fear and crisis during the period in which they confront these issues, make them particularly significant to the experiences of formerly abused women. The barriers to freedom from abuse are the very barriers confronting many women seeking to live without a partner. This suggests that a link exists between the culturally supported gender power hierarchy which in this case exists in the distribution of wealth, and specific cultural contexts which lay the foundation for abuse. As discussed in Chapter 2, the findings presented here support feminist analyses of the connections between a social structure which materially supports the nuclear family and the maintenance of opportunity to enact woman abuse.

Obtaining Medical Aid

Women who have left their abusers often find that they are in need of medical assistance. They may require short-term aid for severe injuries inflicted by their partners. One-tenth of the women interviewed separated from their partners directly after a violent attack and thus were in need of medical help for the injuries they suffered. In addition, women can require aid over time to deal with illnesses that develop from the stressful conditions of their lives, both when they were in relationships and when they are independent from their abuser. For example, in the section above on financial stress, two women explained how they often went without food in order to meet other financial demands. Thus, in addition to the emotional and material problems they confront, women may also be in a position where their basic physical needs are not being met. The women interviewed spoke of physical complaints which sometimes warranted medical attention. Commonly, they described frequent minor illnesses such as colds and flus. They also suffered from infections. For example, one woman who had been repeatedly sexually abused was faced with healing from a debilitating venereal disease which she had contracted from her partner. In addition, women spoke of a general high susceptibility to viruses. At least one-third suffered from rapid weight loss or weight gain and all experienced some level of insomnia, ranging from inability to sleep for the first few nights after leaving to continual or recurring restlessness lasting for up to five years after their relationships had ended.[6]

The interviews revealed large differences between the experiences of British women and US women with respect to medical aid. Only one-tenth of the US women, as compared with eight-tenths of the British women, felt that the health services played a role in their processes of leaving partners and becoming independent. In the US the health services are privatized[7] and thus, unless a woman was receiving state benefit which made her eligible for subsidized medical care or was covered by insurance through her place of employment, medical aid was extremely expensive. As private practitioners could be approached only at a high financial cost, health services did not play a major role in the lives of US women. For many, only when illnesses became acute and impaired their daily lives did they seek medical aid. For example, one woman suffered from a mental breakdown for which she was hospitalized in a psychiatric ward for over a month. She could not function without this hospitalization. Likewise, the woman who suffered from debilitating venereal disease also consulted a doctor. However, women who suffered from recurring colds, flus, insomnia or weight loss or gain dealt with their health problems themselves and used medical remedies available over the counter. Thus, in the US, even for women receiving subsidized care, practitioners were consulted only for specific, necessary medical needs.

Conversely, in Britain, general practitioners (GPs) played a larger role in women's experiences, and they tended to present a variety of needs to them. Because state subsidized health care is available to everyone in Britain, women displayed a different attitude towards seeking medical aid and calling on the expertise of medical authorities. In general, GPs were seen as counsellors or potential sources of support as well as people who could provide physical care. Thus, eight of the eleven women consulted a GP at least once during the period after their relationships with abusers had ended, and their reasons for consultation included both minor and major physical complaints as well as feelings of depression and despair. In this way, the British women's use of medical expertise differed greatly from that of those interviewed in the US.

Because the complaints of British women were so diverse and often entailed a psychological element, GPs were seen as most helpful to them when they provided emotional support. One-half of the women who consulted GPs mentioned that they were most helpful when they counselled rather than prescribed drugs for distress:

> My GP understood and he was brilliant . . . I went to him whenever I wanted to grumble and cry. He would be there.

Thus, depending upon the extent to which individual GPs would address the problems surrounding women's physical illnesses, they were perceived by women to be either helpful or unhelpful.

Correspondingly, the most common complaint about the responses of GPs to the needs of British women concerned the way in which they treated solely physical problems without regard to the surrounding circumstances which contributed to a woman's distress or illness. For example, one-half said that GPs responded to their distress with the suggestion that they take tranquillizers. Although for one woman this interaction occurred over 15 years ago, it appears that this can still be a response of GPs. Two women were prescribed tranquillizers for their distress within two years prior to the interviews. When GPs effectively ignored the emotional and practical problems underlying women's reported experiences of anxiety and depression (that is they prescribed a drug to minimize the symptoms of the problem rather than addressing the root cause), they were felt to be highly unhelpful and, in fact, damaging to women's overall health. These women felt that they needed resolution of the practical and emotional problems they faced, and prescriptions of tranquillizers, although reducing the stress they experienced, also severely impaired their ability to address the conflicts in their lives.

In sum, then, interaction with the medical system was a significant issue for women in the UK. They sought support from GPs which included recognizing the circumstances of abuse which created physical symptoms. To the extent that GPs did this, they were an appropriate source of support and medical care. If they ignored the wider circumstances, in some cases, they exacerbated women's health issues.

Obtaining Protection

Both US and British women expressed a need for safety during the first months to a year after leaving their partners. The abuse they had received, the threat of further abuse from their ex-partners and, in some cases, the first experience of living independently, all contributed to a sense of vulnerability. In fact, contrary to the implications contained in much of the relevant literature,[8] women were vulnerable, and their fears from past experience heightened their sense of this. One-third of the group interviewed experienced an attack, attempted attack, or explicit threat of attack from their ex-partners after leaving them. As a result, and because of their fear of potential attacks, over one-third chose to keep their location unknown to their ex-partners after leaving. Of these, six never recontacted or planned to recontact their abusers.

These women lived in a state of fear of retaliation which was grounded in a detailed knowledge of what their ex-partners were capable of doing. This fear and the very real underlying threat were, for some women, part of their lives for years. For example, one woman described how she received phone calls from her abuser concerning reconciliation and often including verbal abuse for two years after leaving. Thus, leaving the violent relationship does not always free a woman from violence or abuse from her ex-partner, and the fear that results from this possibility.

In response to this threat, women attempted to increase their safety in a variety of ways. They drew on various sources of protection which included personal strategies and those enlisting the help of others. Some examples of these are described below.

One-quarter of the women created invisibility by removing all possibility that they could be tracked to their current addresses by their former partners. Family and friends were advised to claim that they had no knowledge of their whereabouts if asked by former partners. Women went to extreme measures to keep their names out of telephone directories and off post-boxes and door-plates so that their abusers could not come across any sign that they lived in a particular place. Moreover, women described how they paid phone, electricity and gas bills under aliases because they knew that their former partners would adopt extreme measures to attain confidential information from the companies concerned. In this way they essentially removed any indication of their existence from all records which might reveal their addresses.

One-third created a distraction which obscured their location from their ex-partners. One woman, for example, asked her friends and family to tell her partner that she was living in an out of state shelter for battered women whereas, in fact, she had taken up private residence in a nearby city. She hoped that this story, confirmed by everyone she knew, would draw her partner's attention away from her actual residence and towards a futile but complex search amongst shelters whose locations and lists of residents were highly confidential. Another woman created a smoke-screen to distract her former partner by arranging to have neighbours and friends make changes in her home such that it appeared as if she was still living there, while she was actually staying with friends. As a result, the abuser's attacks continued to be directed at the home while the woman remained safe.

In addition, women secured their safety by taking precautions against the possibility of attack. In most cases this entailed carrying weapons. Although extreme and risky in that weapons might be turned against them during an attack, their experiences showed that such precaution could be fruitful. In one case, a US woman carried a handgun and managed to frighten off her abuser when he jumped out of the bushes one morning and attempted to attack her.

The above strategies rely primarily on the creativity and ingenuity of formerly abused women. However, when the threat of violence exceeds a woman's capacity to protect herself, she must seek the help of others. The women interviewed described three sources of external help. Examples of one of these, their families, are already detailed above in terms of creating invisibility and distractions. The other two, refuges and the police, are the subject of this section.

As mentioned above, seven women sought refuge residence. They did so not only because they had nowhere else to live but also because they feared that their partners might attempt to attack them after they had left and they were not sure that they could effectively keep their whereabouts unknown without refuge protection. The refuges in both the US and Britain are highly attentive to the possibility that ex-partners may seek out women. All information about residents and the location of the refuge is completely confidential and staff are trained to be extremely careful of callers who may be surreptitiously trying to gain information. Moreover, refuge staff will move women to other refuges within their networks if there is any indication that abusers may suspect their former partners are staying at a specific one. This complex and well maintained system of security affords women safety from the potential violence.

Secondly, one-half of all the women spoke of involvement with the police at some time after their separation from their partners. Police assistance was available only after women had evidence of attack. Thus their help was largely in dealing with individual cases in which assaults or attempted assaults were in process or had recently occurred. Women called on police protection when they realized that their abusers had discovered their locations and/or when they saw from the behaviour of their abusers that they might intend to commit violence. Half of the women who sought police aid found employment of this strategy resulted in police response which was helpful. Their response was deemed helpful if it included one or more of the following: the police arrived promptly; they diffused the situation or physically protected women from their partners' attacks if an attack was occurring; they removed the abuser or saw that the abuser left the scene and that the women were in temporary safety; they offered advice as to actions women might take against their partners and to secure their safety; they did not take an accusing or prejudicial stance towards the women; and they provided a female officer to document the injuries and statements of the abused woman. By contrast, if the police did not take a woman's account seriously, then the service they offered obviously was experienced as unhelpful and inappropriate. The other half of this group found the police response concerning issues with their ex-partners to be inadequate, reporting amongst other problems that the police would take no action against ex-partners unless they caused evident physical injury to the women. For these women, the requirement of physical harm for police intervention meant that they could not bring institutional forces to bear on the prevention of an assault, regardless of their experienced knowledge about the potential of their former partners to be violent. This denial of protection heightened the sense of vulnerability which originally led these women to seek police aid and, in this sense, worsened their circumstances.[9]

Furthermore, even when a physical assault had been committed, the police did not always take the matter seriously. Half of the women who were dissatisfied with police response reported this. For example, one woman felt that she received inadequate police support because she identified herself as lesbian after separating from her husband. When this was revealed to the police by her family, she found little cooperation in pressing charges against her ex-partner for his assault on their daughter. She perceived that the police blamed her for the violence carried out by her husband because she identified herself as lesbian and she suggested that, because of this, they refused to press charges regardless of the fact that a crime of sexual assault had been committed and proof was available. This woman, then, told how heterosexism impacted her access to appropriate police response. The effect of double oppression on women's access to police aid has been documented by others (Mama, 1989b). For these women, then, even when evidence of assault was offered, their experience of police protection was unsatisfactory.

There is evidence that police policies regarding domestic violence are changing, suggesting that, in time, so will police response. Susan Edwards documented change in the London police which acknowledged that, in police response, 'victims' be transported to safety; new legislation be drafted such that prosecution may proceed even if witnesses are unwilling to support the process; training be enhanced; and the status of work in domestic violence be promoted relative to other police work (Edwards, 1989). Similarly, over the last 10 years, US cities have begun to adopt a mandatory arrest law which requires police to arrest for misdemeanour in cases of domestic violence. Also, in the US at least, some of this problem has been alleviated by court orders available to battered women which mandate that their partners not contact them. Even so, obtaining and enforcing such orders can be problematic and risky. Policy cannot change the attitudes of all police, and to some extent the police response will depend on the individual police involved, as reflected in the experiences here. However, perhaps the more favourable experiences of US women with police reflect the longer-standing US policy changes.

In addition to police response, the legal system can also obstruct women's safety through granting abusers joint custody of children or through creating more dangerous circumstances by requiring drawn-out court proceedings. For example, in one case, a US woman fought her husband's right to access over five separate court battles, only winning her case once a third party testified to the emotional distress suffered by the children when in contact with their father. One-fifth of the total group expressed their frustration with their former abusers' relationships with their children but were required to continue contact with them because they held access rights. The issues underlying this frustration were twofold. First, women felt that, in order to secure their own safety, they needed to arrange complex ways of allowing their former partners to visit. In two of these cases women felt their safety would be in danger if their former abusers were given knowledge about where they lived and so were forced to arrange meetings between the fathers and the children through a third party.

A second issue that arose from their comments was that court rulings granted abusers an opportunity to continue their contact with them. In their view, their former partners used access rights to exercise this opportunity rather than to establish a relationship with their children. The following passage illustrates:

> We came out of court and he kept shouting across the road 'Oh, when can I see my kids?' . . . He's got access. But when he comes, he used to come, he used to come and talk to me.

This discrepancy between court and abuser intent concerning the issue of access rights highlights the dilemma faced by women with children. Court rulings which enforce a father's right to access without consideration of women's safety afford the abuser a tool to continue his harassment of a partner. Moreover, none of the women interviewed sought court injunctions or orders. Barron points out that, because of delays in court proceedings and complications in serving batterers with court papers, women may find themselves in more dangerous circumstances. Periods in which abusers are aware of women's attempts to gain legal protection and such protection has yet to be granted, or is granted but is not respected by abusers, can be extremely dangerous and deter women from seeking court action (Barron, 1990). This may be one reason why the women interviewed chose not to seek protection from the courts.

Thus, although protection is a key issue for formerly abused women, they may not be able to rely on the support of the legal system. Although the legal response to abused women is constantly under pressure from activists, at present formerly abused women are not guaranteed the kind of protection they require despite the fact that they have overcome tremendous obstacles in leaving their abusers.

The Impact of Drastic Change in Circumstances

As discussed above, the practical process of securing a home, financial support, medical care and safety is often fraught with problems and frustration for formerly abused women. At the same time that they address these practical problems they are coping with their emotional responses to the enormous change in circumstances that their action has brought about. Although freeing themselves from abuse was seen by women to be a positive change, the actual emotional process was not experienced without pain. Like any other women who have just ended relationships, the women interviewed experienced a variety of changes such as being suddenly single, living alone, becoming a single parent, and the practical problems addressed above. Because the change was so drastic, women responded at an intense emotional level. They felt some combination of relief, achievement, grief or shock. These are emotions that accompany the practical process and are usually present during the first year or more required for women to achieve a secure independence from their abusers.

At first, some women were overcome with a deep sense of relief that they no longer lived with or were in contact with their abusers. In establishing housing and safety, one-third said relief was the dominant feeling in their lives. Relief was in response to the lessening of the emotional or physical danger, of the need to be constantly vigilant of their partners' moods and behaviour, and of the expenditure of energy in worry, fear and survival. This was a response experienced by women who suffered from an intensity of abuse which shaped their every minute of existence, as illustrated by the following quote:

> Mainly relief first. Absolute relief, that was the biggest thing . . . Just knowing that he wouldn't come in and start yelling at me every night, that he wasn't on the phone.

For women who had not experienced physical violence, escaping from continual emotional abuse was similar:

> Immediately I felt a sense of enormous relief. And I felt like I had finally got away from something.

Regardless of the nature of the abuse that women had suffered, some responded to freedom from day to day emotional or physical threat with immense relief.

Secondly, some women suffered from an acute sense of grief in response to the realization that they were now single. Overwhelmed by the understanding that the partner they had hoped would stop his or her violence would probably continue to be abusive, and by memories of times when their relationships had felt deeply intimate and loving, women felt lonely for their former partners and experienced loss at the end of the relationships. For most of them, five-sixths of the group, this sense of love for their partners had disappeared long before they separated for the final time. Thus grief, although present, was not an immediate, dominant response to leaving. For these women, then, loss is not a central issue. However, particularly for women who left quickly in response to immediate danger, missing their partners during the first few months after separation was immensely painful. For them, the relationship ended because of external intervention, i.e. police arresting and jailing an abuser, or because women feared for their children's and their own lives. Although they feared their partners, they also felt there were positive and intensely intimate aspects of their relationships, and still held hope for change in their partners' abusive behaviour. It was the loss of these positive aspects, and the realization that there was no hope for a healthy relationship, over which women grieved. The intensity at which grieving over this loss was experienced is described below:

> So I went and stayed with my parents again for a couple of days. And the same thing . . . the crying, and me feeling horrible and feeling like my guts were gonna come out my mouth from crying so hard, I missed him *so* badly, and felt so alone and so devastated.

The extremity of this woman's reaction to giving up hope that the intimacy she had shared might continue without abuse mirrors the responses of other women and demonstrates how overwhelming this initial response can be.

A third response to the initial drastic change that accompanies the practical changes outlined previously was described by the women as a feeling of numbness or shock. One-third of the women interviewed felt this was central to their first year after leaving their partners. The combination of practical problems, transition in lifestyle and seemingly conflicting and bewildering emotions (such as both relief and grief) is sometimes too intense to emotionally withstand or acknowledge:

> I noticed for a while I felt real dormant, nothing was going on, cause I was just struggling creating a new life! Creating a home and environment and feeling safe and comfortable, and feeding kids.

In contrast to the intense emotions described in this section, some women responded with numbness and shock during the initial period of establishing their independence. Others fluctuated between intense feelings and periods of numbness in which their ability or desire to feel other feelings was minimal.

Finally, women experienced an initial surge of achievement that, despite the extensive control exerted by their former abusers, the obstacles described above and sometimes meagre financial resources, they were able to escape and survive on their own. As women realized they could cope with living independently and, in fact, managed practical problems better than their partners had, they experienced a sense of competency:

> I think the shock was: not only could I [manage money], but I was doing it a damn sight better than he *ever* did and I had money left over.

Two-thirds of the group found that this financial control gave them a sense of freedom, even when the amount they controlled was barely enough to support them. That they knew how the money was spent, that they decided which bills might go unpaid and why, added to their sense of competency as they realized they were coping. For example, one woman expressed the joy and freedom she felt in being solely in control of her finances:

> I have a choice. It's something I would never give up for the world! I have the choice what I spend my money on. And it's not his money . . . So just having the control is real neat, I like that.

Moreover, one-quarter experienced an actual rise in their standard of living, which, although the standard was still low, was better in comparison to the stressful economic position imposed by abusers. This is not to say that these women who have left abusers did not suffer financially. That they encounter many difficulties and economic distress is confirmed above. What is important is that the amount of financial distress they experienced after leaving their abusers was, for some, significantly less than that which they experienced as a result of the deprivation enforced by their partners. In this sense, economic independence was liberating, even when independence required that women live on the minimum income of state benefit.

More importantly, the discovery of unexpected talents and proficiencies in coping with independent life combated the lowered self-esteem that women carried out of their relationships. Often women were controlled through economic deprivation and told by their partners that they could not be trusted with more money because they were unable to manage finances:

> Not just that I could stand up to this guy, leave him, turns out he's just this scared little boy who's afraid of me, and I have all this power. It was like '*yeah*! I *survived* that!'

Thus, in recognizing their achievement over the many problems they face in leaving abusive partners, women continue to shift the balance of power between them and their former partners. As discussed in Chapter 4, women used some of their emotional responses to shift the power imbalance in their relationships. That that shift was successful enough to allow them to leave does not imply that they have completely regained their full sense of power over their own lives. This shift continues after they have left their partners. Moreover, they do not stop feeling the emotions of anger and fear which enabled them to begin creating this shift of power. As we will see in the following chapter, the themes of fear and anger emerge again, just as the theme of shifting power has above. We keep returning to these themes, like the women themselves did during the interviews, as each aspect of experience sheds light on the complex issue involved. Outward movement along the spiral continues beyond leaving abusive partners. At each instance of return to an issue, women gain new insight into the impact of these responses on their lives, and move towards greater freedom from abuse.

Thus, women spoke of vast fluctuations in their feelings of grief, relief and shock in response to the dramatic change of circumstances in their lives and with which they had to cope in order to carry out their daily or weekly activities such as working, caring for children, or securing housing or government financial aid. By far the most effective strategy of coping is described by women as taking one day at a time, or one hour at a time, depending on the intensity of their emotions. Because the fluctuations between numbness and intense emotion were unpredictable, women found that they needed to take each fluctuation as it came and focus on the positive periods in order to bear the painful ones:

> One day at a time is exactly how you do it. Because you have days when you could take on the world and you have days when you feel like you're in Dante's inferno, and you can barely get out of bed . . . You barely get up and get the kids dressed and fed . . . And I still have days like that . . . and then I have other days where, I could do anything and I sort of cling to them because I know the next day could be another day where I'm dog tired and miserable.

By doing this, she felt she could survive the most painful days. Other women concentrated on practical issues in order to lessen their awareness of pain. Their preoccupation with the stress of securing housing, finances, medical aid and protection took precedence over the feelings about having been abused and they were able to sort out daily problems and minimize the surge of feelings threatening to overwhelm them. The potential for being overwhelmed by an intense roller coaster of emotions contrasts with the alternative of a numbness characterized by lack of feelings. The potential for either state requires that women create coping mechanisms in order to continue functioning. As we will see, however, ultimately women must create a safe arena for feeling the intense emotions described here and in the next chapter. Neither numbness nor coping with intense fluctuations of feeling serves as a satisfactory basis for living, in the longer term.

In conclusion, this chapter has shown that the obstacles faced by the women in meeting their needs presented a complicated and diverse set of problems. The 'solution' of leaving an abuser, then, was only a first step in a long process of establishing physical separation and emotional autonomy from abusers. Within this process both British and US women created their own individual route in which they found the information they required and continued to assert their needs through sometimes lengthy negotiations with the service agencies or people to whom they went for help. Moreover, in meeting their needs for housing, money, medical aid and protection, women demonstrated a variety of creative solutions in the face of a dearth of resources. The initial change in circumstances, and the practical problems in creating this, have their emotional impact on women. They feel a combination of relief, grief, numbness and achievement which interacts with their concurrent emotional process of healing from abuse. In the following chapters, I will address personal healing and the transition from being abused to becoming free from abuse. This is the side of transition which, rather than consisting of practical change and the emotions which accompany it, deals with the inner change towards overcoming the impact of abuse. Yet, as we will see, this inner change is affected by external conditions and thus is interrelated with women's social and cultural circumstances.

Notes

1 Marin, in an unpublished MA thesis on battered women who had left their partners, suggested that, within the first year after leaving a refuge, women in a British city found that housing and finance played a major role in their lives. She noted the trauma of waiting for housing or rehousing by the council, the bleakness of emergency shelter, and the low standard of housing, in general, in which the women she interviewed resided. She also expressed the problems women encountered, as did those in this study, with finding employment and applying for state financial aid (Marin, 1985). Likewise, Lee Ann Hoff carried out a study of social network responses to nine US battered women who had resided in refuges during the first year after they left their partners. Unlike my research, her focus was primarily on the answers of support network members to questionnaires and interviews about their responses to the women, rather than on the women's own experiences and their reactions. However, she did note that many of the problems confronted by the nine women during the first year of separation concerned securing adequate housing and finances. Finally, Jan Pahl (1985b) has cited such practical problems as a major factor in women's decisions to return to their partners. Thus other studies, which focus only on the initial experiences of women who have left partners or those who have stayed in refuges, confirm the experiences of the women in this research: that they are confronted with problematic circumstances concerning the availability of housing and finances both when they are in the relationship and once they leave it.

2 One exception to this is Hoff's work, in which she hinted that a few women had been contacted through public health networks rather than refuges, but did not specify for how many of the nine this was true.

3 Four of the women interviewed had been independent from their abusers for over 10 years at the time of the interviews. For them, refuges were few or non-existent at the time they left their partners. Thus their experiences do not form part of this discussion of refuge services.

4 There are some differences between those services provided in the US and those in Britain. First, the Women's Aid, which is the largest and best known network of British refuges, and which housed some of the women interviewed for this research, has some policies that differ from the US refuges belonging to a national network called the National Coalition Against Domestic Violence. For instance, in the Women's Aid refuges, policy demands that women who contact the refuge and are leaving partners as a result of abuse, either physical or emotional, are offered space if it is available. There seems to be much less negotiation with women before they are offered space than in the US. As a result, women in Britain had little problem attaining refuge space if they requested it, but they found their living conditions to be extremely overcrowded. Both from the interviews with US women and from my experience of working in a US shelter, it is clear that shelters in the US may explore a number of options with women in order to ascertain that she is in danger, has no other options but to stay at a refuge and would find refuge life acceptable. The reason for this careful assessment is to reserve the limited refuge space for those women who are most in need.

5 These figures were based on women's finances for 1989.

6 Other researchers have also suggested that health services complicate the problems of women in relationships with abusive partners. Stark and Flitcraft explored the response of American health systems. They discovered that women who sought medical attention for injuries inflicted by their partners were identified as abused in only 4 per cent of the 1300 cases. Instead, their injuries were reported by doctors as 'a series of unfortunate accidents' (Stark et al., 1982: 31) and the various secondary problems arising from abuse were, in many cases, diagnosed as symptoms of women's personal pathologies. Likewise, Dobash and Dobash found that UK doctors frequently responded to battered women's stress by prescribing tranquillizers (Dobash and Dobash, 1980). The finding in research on battered women that doctors treat the symptoms of stress rather than its causes is not uncommon (Martin, 1978; Pagelow, 1981a). Stark et al., (1979; 1982) forward an argument in which the widespread existence of inappropriate medical approaches to battered women leads to a second victimization of them by health services. Thus the women in my research who were prescribed tranquillizers, in order to cope with the stresses faced in leaving their partners, experienced a medical response which is commonly confronted by women who have not left their abusers.

7 In the United States patients pay for their medical bills without government assistance, unless they are receiving state benefit as a sole source of income. In the former case most people attain medical insurance either from their work or individually, as payment for medical services is extremely expensive. However, according to the specifics of the policy, payment of fees may or may not be covered by the insurance, and most policies require evidence of a specific medical problem. Thus approaching a doctor with problems that are not directly related to physical ailments may require that individuals pay high consultation fees. Likewise, when medical aid is subsidized by the government, policies are similar to those of insurance policies and require that a patient suffers from a specific physical ailment when requesting such aid.

8 There is an abundance of literature which follows the experience of battered women to the point at which they leave their relationships. Such literature, which was reviewed in Chapter 1, centres on an implied assumption that the battering ends when

the relationship ends, that battered women cease to be battered once they leave their abusers. This study contradicts that assumption and reveals that ending the relationship does not always mean that a woman is safe from assault.

9 Other research has addressed the role of police intervention in woman abuse. Dobash and Dobash explained how the police were trained to avoid arresting an abuser and that the women they interviewed experienced the police response to their situation as inadequate and sometimes hostile (Dobash and Dobash, 1980). Similarly, other researchers have described how the police failed to protect women from abusers when they were in relationships (Martin, 1976; Pagelow, 1981a; Pizzey, 1974). Susan Schechter (1982) described how the US battered women's movement took as one of its primary aims the restructuring of police policy and responses to battered women, implying that both were inappropriate and in some cases harmful in their approaches to woman abuse.

6

The Impact of Abuse and the Context in which Formerly Abused Women Seek Healing

Women's experiences of having been abused and their circumstances after leaving an abuser have a much longer impact than do women's immediate responses to practical change. In the long term, anger and fear are part of the spiral of freeing oneself from abuse that exists after relationships have ended, in that they are not constantly felt but rather re-emerge as women move towards greater freedom from abuse and healing. These two issues, then, will form the basis for the first half of this chapter.

It is important to note also that the loss of control described in Chapter 4 is not completely restored from the moment a woman is free from abuse. Particularly, women described the long-term reconstruction of their identity and self-esteem as a continual recognition and rejection of the damaging messages about themselves instilled by their abusers. These themes, identity and self-esteem, re-emerge in this chapter and the next as part of the process of healing from abuse. In the second half of this chapter I will address women's perceptions of popular beliefs and media images, which formed a context for their struggle to heal and which often triggered many of the feelings they held about having been abused or having left abusers.

The Impact of Abuse and Leaving Abusers

Fear
Although women left their abusers, the impact of continual harassment, emotional injury and the threat or enactment of physical violence could not be shaken off instantaneously and, in a number of ways, continued to haunt and resurface. In addition to resurfacing fear, women also felt fear of actual assault in the future – either from their former partners or in new relationships that could potentially be abusive. In the interviews, women described fear in two general ways: day to day tension and anxiety marking a kind of generalized fear,[1] and periods of acute, overwhelming fear.

The first of these, generalized fear, was described by five-sixths of the women to be present in their lives for periods of months or years.

During these times, fear or anxiety was so continually present that it became part of women's day to day reality. The lived experience of this was described as jumpiness or constant vague worry:

> For a long time I was *real* jumpy and people would walk up to me, I didn't know they were there and [I would] gasp. I was doing that a lot, kinda hyper.

> Underneath I'm working on this level really, I'm feeling all the time like 'What's gonna happen next?' . . . 'What *could* happen next?'

Although different, what is central to these expressions of generalized fear is a sense of the vulnerability that permeated women's perceptions and reactions to their circumstances. The fear that something drastic may happen to them at any minute, that they must be ever vigilant of impending danger in order to protect their safety, was the emotional state forced upon them during the time they were abused. This was a necessary response to abuse, because if a woman was not ever vigilant of danger she might fail to see the warning signs of an attack, if any were present, and thus lose the opportunity to protect herself. When the threat of abuse becomes lethal, as it was for many of the women in this study, then this vigilant anxiety is literally a tool of survival; a lapse may result in severe damage or death. Given the seriousness of maintaining such vigilance, it is not surprising that, even once the impending threat of violence was not present, women carried with them a sense of intense vulnerability.

This was particularly an issue for women who wanted to be or were in new relationships. The possibility of being abused again and the association of intimacy with their experiences of abuse elicited a deep fear in women about being involved in a new relationship. Two-thirds of the women feared a new partner would turn out to be abusive and this fear permeated their current lives:

> There's always the fear that you're gonna get back into the relationship again. If not with him then with somebody else.

Part of generalized fear, then, was rooted in the possibility that abuse could occur in the future.

Likewise, as described in the previous chapter, women may be unsure of their safety from future attack from their former abusers. Women who severed relations with their former abusers in order to secure their emotional and physical safety were more than aware that they could not predict when they might come in contact with their former abusers, either by accident or because their abusers might track them to their new location. For these women, generalized fear was related to their present circumstances and not entirely related to resurfacing feelings, although their past experiences of fear certainly lent depth to current feelings. The fear of potential attack was potent to women because they were extensively knowledgeable about the violence and brutality of which their partners were capable.

A second type of fear of which women spoke can be described as periodic, overwhelming terror, consisting of resurgence of the terror women had experienced when they were being abused. With regard to this, women experienced two types of periodic episodes of extreme fear: nightmares and vivid memories or flashbacks. Both kinds were touched off by circumstances in the present lives of women and both were experienced as a reliving of their pasts, reminding women of the profound effect abuse had on their lives and emotional states.

One-half of the women spoke of nightmares. Although these decreased in frequency over time, they could continue to occur years after the end of the relationships. The substance of women's nightmares entailed actual events that had occurred when they were abused or, more commonly, unrelated content which embodied the terror and anger they felt when abused. These were often triggered by events in the present. For example, two women told me they had nightmares after being interviewed. They thought that the retelling of their experiences triggered these dreams:[2]

> I had a great deal of them after we split up. At that time my nightmare was that I was in a concentration camp with my mother and there was a chance to escape but we had to run across a no man's land that was patrolled by dogs, and jump a barbed wire fence . . . I made it safely into the forest and they couldn't find me but they got my mother . . . I have this nightmare over and over again.

This terrifying image of suffering and life-threatening danger of the most inhumane kind reflected the terror she felt in the relationship with her abuser.

Similarly, vivid memories or flashbacks were experienced by one-half of the women as a kind of reliving of the abuse. They were described by women as if they were back in a specific event in which they were abused, or were experiencing the reaction they used to feel when they were abused. Flashbacks could be extremely painful and intense emotional experiences. One woman explained the level of terror she experienced when her new partner teasingly put a pillow over her face:

> Something real primal says: 'Last time this happened you almost died. So stop it now.' Even though somebody else might joke around with something that might be equally potentially dangerous, if he didn't do that to me, I don't react that way.

Thus one trigger for flashbacks is any re-enactment of the circumstances under which women were abused. This could occur from the behaviour of a new partner or from abuse depicted in a film or a television programme. Likewise, physical surroundings, especially if women chose to live in the accommodation they had previously shared with their abusers, could be a potent trigger:

> And every once in a while, like if I'm thinking about him, and thinking about what happened, if I walk into the kitchen I can kinda feel it, because that was the place where a lot of the physical abuse took place.

This relation between past fear and present circumstances, and the unpredictability of flashbacks, signals to women that they can never be certain that they are completely free from their subjective experiences of abuse. Although they were struggling to leave their past experiences behind and create a new life, flashbacks plunged women into reliving the abuse and reopened the wounds of fear that time may have begun to heal. Even more painful was the fact that the very details of the new lives they were building could serve as agents for triggering this reliving of the past. Because of the unpredictability of what will serve as a trigger for flashbacks, some women felt that this type of periodic fear interfered with their daily lives:

> I get memory flashbacks, like for some reason, all of a sudden it'll be like I'm living it again and there's a couple of real horrendous ones that are just *horrendous*. And I mean it's like reliving it. It's not just a memory, it's like my *whole body* remembers, and that's hard. For six weeks I couldn't sleep . . . I lay down and all of a sudden all I could do was *remember*.

For this woman, then, flashbacks severely impaired her day to day functioning.

In sum, whether fear is experienced on a day to day underlying level or in periods of acute and overwhelming upsurges, women felt that the emotion had a serious impact on their efforts to leave the past behind and to function on a practical level.

Anger

The experience of anger for formerly abused women is multi-levelled and multi-faceted. I described in Chapter 4 how women use anger to fuel their action in leaving. Yet, for many women this would have been the first time that they felt the depth of their rage. In order to cope daily with abuse, most women cannot fully recognize or reveal their anger to their partners without further endangering themselves. It is precisely because their anger so potently threatens the stronghold of control maintained by their partners that its expression may prompt the response of escalated attacks from abusers in an attempt to regain control. So, once women have freed themselves from the danger that prohibited them from fully recognizing their anger, they are often overwhelmed and confused by the depth of rage that surfaces. The anger women described was focused at two issues: the fact that they had been abused; and the current circumstances with which they coped as a result of having to leave an abusive partner. Moreover, there were a number of ways in which anger was experienced by women, some of which were readily identifiable to the women, and some which, only in retrospect, could women define as anger.[3]

As women begin to move out of the web, they see the abuse more and more clearly in its full complexity, subtlety and destructiveness. As this awareness grows, so does their anger at what their abuser has done to them. The anger some women feel in leaving may be in response to the first sense that a deep injustice is being committed against them, and it is usually just a portion of the full rage women eventually discover within themselves. Women who leave in fear also begin to uncover deep anger when it is safe to do so. This anger is part of the shift of power that occurs after women leave. It marks women's transition into believing that they do not deserve to be abused and fully recognizing the extent of abuse they suffered. Despite this, it is a painful and sometimes overwhelming emotion for formerly abused women, even more so because in the past anger might have led to increased danger from their abusers:

> Well some of the things I've told you brings a lot of memories up . . . It's a lot of anger, cause of all the things he's done! It's just bottled up inside me. I just wanna hit at him, I wanna hit at him or out at somethin'.

Moreover, the degree of rage may be overwhelming to women. Women interviewed often felt that their anger at their abusers or about the abuse threatened to obscure their feelings about other aspects of their lives. Like the woman quoted below, they struggled with moving in and out of being in touch with their rage:

> I could get in touch with my anger. But, it was too overwhelming and I had to back away. Cause I had so much anger that I couldn't see anything else beyond that, all I could see was how angry I was.

Anger at abusive partners, then, was a central, sometimes overwhelming or threatening, feeling for formerly abused women.

In addition to this focus, women also felt anger about the circumstances with which they were coping as a result of having to leave an abusive partner. One of these, described by half of the women interviewed, was the relative impoverishment they suffered in comparison with the people who had abused them. For example, women spoke about how they were living in cramped government housing or low priced flats, subsisting on barely enough income to manage the house and feed their children, while their former partners were living in the homes they had shared with an income sufficient to support comfortable living and without the responsibility of rearing children:

It's hard when you see him havin' life so much easier. And he's the one who caused all the problems supposedly.

Moreover, when an abuser was seen to go unpunished for what women were beginning to recognize as extreme and damaging abuse, women felt a deep sense of injustice and anger. One interviewee, for example, felt that people who injured animals were punished more by society and the justice system than were those who abused their partners:

Even now, I think about some of the things . . . he did. I read about those things that youths have done to animals, and they've been jailed for it. And I think God! He's got away with so much!

This sense of injustice is one underlying factor in women's sense of anger at present circumstances.

Women also experience anger as they recognize the impact abuse has on their lives. Not only may they be living on low incomes and substandard housing, but they are also living with the ongoing personal impact that abuse has. As women began to recognize that they suffered from intense fear and low self-esteem after leaving their partners, they felt anger about those personal changes. For example, because of her fear of being abused, one woman felt she was far less able to be intimate with others than she had been previous to her relationship with an abuser:

feeling really alone . . . I really resent him putting me in that position. Cause I'm a very affectionate sort of person and I think, look at what he's done, he's wasted half my adult life really.

Another common anger-provoking change was the experience of depression which women described to be a result of abuse and which often overshadowed their lives.

There was a number of ways in which women expressed anger once it began to surface. Usually, women could not act on their desire for revenge on their partners because they did not want further contact with their abusers or were unwilling to complicate the tenuous relations between their children and former partners. Apart from venting rage directly at their former abusers, women described three ways in which they thought their anger was released indirectly. The first two – anger at children who reminded women of their former partners, and depression – were not seen by women to be positive. The third, however – using anger to make change – was described as a positive way to use their feelings.

One-quarter of the women voiced the problem that their children reminded them of their former partners, because of physical or behavioural similarities, and thus triggered angry feelings about abuse:

> And he was violent, you see. That didn't help because . . . he was a constant source of a reminder of his dad. Everything he did, every action, every blaze of his eyes, every violent thing he did, which was constant.

Because this woman and the others were forced to care daily for children who put them in touch with their anger about past experiences and, in some cases, to have contact with their former partners because they shared children, they felt they could not escape the anger they held inside; yet they desperately did not want to vent this rage at their children, who they recognized were not responsible for the feelings they held. The constancy of reminders, however, was difficult if not impossible to withstand, and women spoke with deep guilt about the rage that leaked out:

> As I say, he was a lot like his dad. That had a lot to do with it because I thought 'well he's gonna be around, I'm gonna be reminded of *that* every day' . . . I used to have problems to do with my [former] boyfriend, I'd look at [my son] and think 'this is all because of you!' I put all the blame on him.

Women recognized that this way of expressing rage was damaging to their children and unhealthy for themselves. They sought to resolve this through counselling or giving full or joint care of their children to their partners, if these partners were not abusive to children. In these latter circumstances, where rage endangered their relationships with their children and this solution seemed to be the only relief to the tension they experienced, giving up a child to an abuser was extremely painful to women. But such a solution was preferable to venting irrepressible rage on children who were coping with abuse issues themselves.

Women also thought that periods of depression related to the rage they felt. In retrospect, women explained that they were deeply angry but unable to acknowledge or feel their anger and, consequently, became immersed in depression. For one-quarter of the women, this depression was so extreme that they seriously contemplated suicide. Rather than recognizing the responsibility of the abuser in creating the circumstances of their lives, these women looked inward for a reason for the trauma and problems they coped with, and thus, rather than feeling anger, thought they were failures and felt despair:

> I thought . . . I can just take the pills . . . I'll die, it'll be all right, I'll die. You know, I just felt so low. I really did feel a total failure and I didn't want to live, I just didn't. I thought: I failed the kids, I failed [my ex-partner] and I failed myself.

In coping with the trauma of leaving an abuser and healing from abuse, particularly because abuse often entails blaming women for conflict in the relationship, formerly abused women may turn the anger inwards and blame themselves for the consequences of abuse.

A final, and most positive, way women expressed their anger was in making change in their lives. In Chapter 7 I will describe the process and levels of change women create in greater detail. However, I want to mention briefly here that such change, just as breaking free from abusers, is often fuelled by anger. In this way, anger is a healthy reaction to abuse; it is a declaration by women that they did not deserve the abuse and its impact, and thus can be a vital key to transformation in women's lives:

> There was anger. But I think I needed to focus on that because I tend to focus on all the good parts. Like when I met him for the weekend. It was such a good weekend. Then on the drive back I had time to say 'Hey, this is an artificial situation. He's demonstrated nothing's changed as far as going to therapy' . . . I did need to focus on the rotten parts of that period.

In this way, anger motivated women to protect their freedom from abuse, even when they missed the attractive and desirable traits of the former partner, and thus was a powerful reinforcement of women's hard earned independence.

Anger which initiated positive change, then, contributed to the growth and healing of formerly abused women. However, it is important to note that this form of expression only occurred once anger was no longer experienced as overwhelming. Channelling anger for positive use required skill and, to some extent, ability to control the rage that surfaced. All of the women interviewed expressed their anger in a variety of ways, including those that were thought to be less healing and those that were more so. It is only once women became less overwhelmed by anger that they were able to channel it for positive change.

In the last chapter, we saw how practical change and the external circumstances under which women seek housing, finances and protection had an impact on women's emotions. In this chapter, thus far, we have examined the emotional impact of abuse in terms of women's feelings of fear and anger which persist after their relationships have ended. These also are related to external circumstances in that the context in which women define themselves as formerly abused women and strive to untangle the complexity of their feelings sometimes presents obstacles. In the second half of this chapter, we will look at some of the obstacles women face, presented by popular beliefs and media representations, in moving through the process of healing from the impact of abuse.

Media Representations, Popular Beliefs and Values: the Impact on Women Healing from Abuse

Throughout the interviews, women tried to explain to me the complexity of their experience of the web of emotional abuse, its long-term impact and the problems of freeing themselves from abuse. In articulating these issues, they returned continually to the impact of the ideas and views about abuse held by others, which exacerbated and contributed generally to the problems they faced in rebuilding their lives.

The women I interviewed found that they encountered a number of popular beliefs about relationships and abuse which contrasted with their experiences, or framed their experiences in a negative perspective. At the point in women's lives when they struggled with enormous emotional and practical issues, they needed from others and from their culture both support for their current struggle and affirmation of their past experiences. As discussed in Chapter 5 and in the section above, there are a number of ways in which women were supported by friends and family – either in terms of assistance in accommodation or finances or in terms of non-judgemental, respectful listening and understanding. What has not been addressed, and yet forms a central theme to the interviews, is the much wider set of stereotypes which recurringly became issues when women tried to explain to me their experiences.

This section is not based on an analysis of the media themselves or on the attitudes of friends, families and potential support networks. The latter has already been explored in a US study (Hoff, 1990). Instead, this chapter looks at how formerly abused women perceive such beliefs, images and values. It asks what is most salient about the attitudes they encounter and what impact such encounters have on them.

Women described three major sources of contradictory or negative attitudes from others which affected them: the media, specifically their experiences of films, television talk shows, situation comedies and advertisements, and newspaper and magazine articles; the reactions of friends and family in terms both of an acceptance of media images and of more general values concerning marriage and heterosexual relationships; and the responses from the potential support networks of specific communities. Women's experiences with anger and fear, as described above, and grief, shock and relief, described in Chapter 5, were often confusing and overwhelming. Furthermore, the isolation and diminished sense of self-identity reinforced by abuse, as described in Chapters 3 and 4, haunted women after they left their abusers. The combination of all this made defining their experiences extremely difficult. Yet, in looking outward to the beliefs and representations presented by others, rather than gaining affirmation of what they strove to define, women became even more confused and unsure of their experience, which compounded the obstacles and trauma they already faced.

Media Representations of Abuse

When women wanted to gain a perspective on their experiences, they were attracted to articles or programmes which addressed the issue of 'battered women' or abusive relationships. Nearly all the women spoke of a deep desire to find out more about abuse and violence in relationships, in the hope that they might understand their own experiences more clearly. When asked whether they had come across any material that was helpful, and what sources they had sought, many responded with frustration about the type of information that was readily available, especially on television, in films, and in magazines and newspapers. They felt that, in comparison with their own experiences, most of the information they encountered was inappropriate, judgemental or stereotyped, and was not relevant to their own experiences. Although not all information encountered was viewed in this way, that which was thought to be helpful was normally found in book form, was very scarce and had to be actively sought.[4] The majority of popular and easily acceptable information in the media was not affirming. Specifically, women identified two ways in which the images they encountered in the media were inappropriate, stereotyped and contradictory, and thus prevented them from gaining the affirmation they sought through these sources. These ways were sensationalistic approaches to physical violence, and the depiction of emotional abuse as erotic or humorous.

The predominant representation women felt they encountered about abuse was that of the 'battered wife'. Television programmes and newspaper or magazine articles were described by the women interviewed as portraying a stereotyped and unbalanced image of abuse. Women described the stereotypes to consist of rigid, recurring characteristics of battered women by exclusive focusing only on the physical abuse. 'Battered women', according to the popular images in the media which women encountered, were heterosexual, married, working class mothers and were subjected to extreme physical abuse. Less than a quarter of the women interviewed might be said to fit this description and, even for them, identification with this image was not straightforward. Women said that their experiences of abuse could not be defined or measured in terms of the number of bruises or injuries they incurred. In the opinion of many of them, media depictions of this kind were exploitative and sensationalized. When questioned, women remarked that such programmes drew upon the most gory details of violence, to the exclusion of exploring the emotional and practical aspects of women's experiences – much in the same way that a horror film would seek to attract viewers. Some of these women had experienced extreme physical violence and they insisted that public awareness that such violence could be enacted by a partner was important. But to convey this information without respect for the emotional aspects of abuse was contrary to these women's experiences.

Consequently, conflicting and inaccurate images of abuse caused them to question the accuracy of their own experiences of it, and thus their own identity as abused women. This challenge to identity mirrors and compounds the impact of abuse on women's identity (see Chapter 4):

> But since they only show the worst cases, it's really easy to say 'I'm not battered, because that didn't happen to me.'

The lack of focus on the emotional dimension of abuse, then, combined with a sensationalized view of physical violence and stereotyped characteristics of 'battered women', was detrimental to women's efforts to define and believe their own experiences of abuse. Moreover, in being unsure of their identity as formerly abused women, they are also unsure of the justifiability of their anger and fear about the abuse (Kelly, 1988a).

Women also told how the emotional aspects of abuse shown on television or in films were depicted as humorous or erotic – part of the tension or dynamics between lovers that contributes to intense sexual passion. In contrast to the shocking and grotesque approach to physical abuse, emotional abuse is shown to be acceptable or even desirable. For example, one woman described how television situation comedies often based humour on an exchange of insults or a tangled web of deceptions and lies between partners:

> I watch sitcoms sometimes . . . their main type of humour is to abuse each other, 'well you're this, well you're that, you stupid' . . . however they phrase it. And that can bring memories back.

This woman was confused and distressed about the intensity of her own reactions to the memories triggered by these representations which, in being painful and distressing, did not match the humorous tone of the programmes.

In addition, women described the ways in which they perceived the media to celebrate and eroticize abuse. One woman expressed this as follows:

> I went to see *9½ Weeks*, this movie. It just wiped me out . . . they showed him slapping her a little bit, but it was almost sexual and there was no bruises, and the humiliation. So that upset me, they made it so attractive.

For this woman, the film *9½ Weeks* demonstrated much of the behavioural reality of her own experience with abuse, but celebrated this behaviour by eroticizing it. Although the actions of the couple in the film were similar to her experience, the emotions she felt in response to this abuse were not depicted. The dynamics of the relationship were shown as erotic. The physical violence of slapping was depicted as desirable as it was used to illustrate the intensity of emotion in the sexual relationship of the couple in the film. Rather than showing a process in which, as a result of abuse, women were gradually being increasingly controlled and were losing their self-esteem and identity, the focus was on desire as a drive so powerful that women disregarded, or even enjoyed, the destructive nature of the relationship. Dworkin and McKinnon have argued that the eroticization of abuse forms the foundation of pornography and is oppressive to women (Dworkin, 1981; McKinnon, 1992). Moreover, recent works have also noted that women have specific and potent responses to media representations of violence (Schlessinger et al., 1992). Like images that treated abuse as humorous, these confused women about how their experience of abuse and its painful impact fitted into a culture which sees emotional control as erotic.

Negative Responses from Friends and Family

Women also seek or are confronted by the perspectives of friends and family. In specific cases, women talked of an individual family member or friend who was extremely supportive in facilitating them to explore and understand their own experiences. Examples of the acts of such people were given in Chapters 4 and 5 and earlier in this chapter. However, much more commonly women remarked 'people just don't understand what it's like'. They described over and over again how 'people' refused to believe that they had been abused, or pressurized women to adopt values which contradicted their experiences. When the women were questioned, 'people' were revealed to be personal friends, family, coworkers and acquaintances. The sum of their social contacts was represented, in the women's view, as a uniform group in terms of their lack of understanding of the nature of their experiences.

Because women were sometimes overwhelmed by their emotions, the affirmation from a friend or family member that what they were feeling was an appropriate and acceptable response to what they had suffered would have allowed them to accept, and thus explore more fully, their feelings about both physical and emotional abuse and leaving an abuser. When they did receive it, in fact, this type of support gave women the strength to begin to trust their own understanding of what occurred and thus to begin to rebuild their self-esteem and sense of identity.

Yet, in the majority of women's experiences, friends or family members simply refused to accept that women had been abused, usually because the women did not meet up to the stereotype they held about 'battered women'. It is noteworthy that, although some women had been out of their relationships for over 15 years, a period in which much public attention and social action has focused on the issue of 'battered women' (Schechter, 1982), the themes that arose from their early experiences did not differ drastically from those of women who had left within a few years of the time of the interviews. Thus, despite the changes that have taken place, the issues in this chapter are still part of the experiences of formerly abused women.

When women described their experiences, expressed their feelings about having been abused or related why the abuse had such a long-lasting impact upon them, they were often faced with disbelief or rejection of the reality of their experiences and feelings. This was particularly true for women who had suffered little or no physical abuse. Because they did not fit into the commonly held stereotypes about 'battered women', these women found that their pain was trivialized by friends. For example, a woman who had been emotionally abused by her lover remarked: ' "Well she didn't hit you did she?" was the response I got a lot.' Immediate comparison was drawn between her and the image of a 'battered wife' held by her friends. Because she didn't meet up to the stereotype of a woman who had been physically assaulted, her experience of abuse was dismissed.

In addition, women said that, within a few months after leaving their partners, most friends and family members got tired of hearing about abuse and the impact it had had. Rather than simply saying that they no longer wanted to hear about it, they encouraged the women to see their feelings as inappropriate, as making too much out of the situation, and as something to be left behind in order for them to 'get on with' their lives. In this way, friends and family compounded the problem by not only refusing to acknowledge and respect the emotions of formerly abused women but also asserting that these emotions were inappropriate.

Women also found that some friends or family avoided the topic of abuse. They neither mentioned the relationship nor responded with interest when women brought up the subject. Women described how they would say something minor about their experience, in order to see whether others would support their need to talk. A common response to this consisted of a blank look and a change in subject, signalling to women that they were unwilling to accept the existence and impact of the abuse women had experienced.

All three of these ways of refusing to acknowledge the abuse or its impact had a potent effect on women. Usually, when confronted with such responses, women simply stopped talking about their experiences, because they knew that they would not receive the kind of support and acceptance they sought. However, as women were confronted with a refusal to accept again and again, their experiences of abuse in which partners continually questioned the accuracy of their perceptions were mirrored. Thus women's sense of distorted reality, resulting from abuse and persisting after their relationships had ended, was compounded.

Moreover, there was a variety of ways that the responses of others affected a woman's self-esteem and compounded the issues she already faced with regard to self-esteem. For example, one woman spoke about her feelings when she told other people about her experiences:

> Oh extremely embarrassed. And depending on how embarrassed or uncomfortable I feel about it, I will go away feeling 'Oh God that was a real mistake, what am I complaining about anyway?' I get confused about what my own experience is.

These feelings are symptomatic of a low sense of self-worth, i.e. that the desire to express and sort through experiences of pain and emotional trauma is actually 'complaining'. The word 'complain' trivialized the process of recovery this woman was undergoing.

As a whole, such responses made women extremely wary of revealing any aspect of their experiences, as they wanted to avoid the blatant refusal to accept that abuse had occurred and had had a significant impact on their lives. Women often continued to test for the receptiveness of others by revealing minor, subtle aspects of their experiences of abuse. However, many became silenced and wary about seeking out those individuals who might have offered the support and acceptance they desired.[5]

The Impact of Group Oppression on the Responses of Alternative Support Groups

In addition to the experiences described above, women also discussed negative responses they encountered from alternative potential support groups working together to fight a common oppression. Although this section is based on the responses of three women, the issues they raised inform the challenges to feminist theories made by lesbians and black women, as outlined in Chapter 1. Thus their experiences have a particular importance to feminist analysis and are worth emphasis.[6]

In discussing the images and values women see portrayed on television and in the media, I have been focusing on the representations created by the dominant groups in society. Women also sought support from groups to which they were racially, culturally or politically allied – groups which would not be expected to hold the same perspectives and values as the dominant groups. These alternative potential support groups often hold in common social knowledge about how they are oppressed by the images produced by white heterosexual culture and thus would seem to offer an avenue of support for formerly abused women who find themselves at odds with the images they encounter.

First, the two US women interviewed who had been abused in lesbian relationships felt that the responses of women from the domestic violence movement to abused lesbians were extremely negative at the time they left their partners.[7] For example, one woman spoke of her involvement with the US battered women's movement during the time she lived with the woman who abused her:

> There was such a black and white mentality, that abusers are men and they are bad people and abused women are women and they are good people and women are good people and men are bad people . . . it was a real dichotomized kinda picture . . . if I acknowledged what was happening in this relationship, that would be labelling this person who I had a lot of respect for in a lot of ways, who was a political ally of mine, as a bad person and thereby discounting all the good things about her.

As a result of the movement's simplistic perspective, which was created to challenge the stereotype that heterosexual 'battered women' are deviant, abused lesbians spoke of being received with hostility when they identified their partner's abusive behaviour. Until recently in the US and very recently in the UK (Kelly et al., 1989; Kelly, 1991), with a growing discussion of abuse in lesbian relationships, the challenge to general cultural stereotypes has been protected at the cost of examining the complexities of woman abuse. As a result, lesbian women who had left abusive partners encountered a variety of negative responses from groups which otherwise supported and affirmed the experiences of women who had been abused.

Secondly, these two women from lesbian relationships interviewed for this study related that a major issue they confronted also lay in the responses of lesbians within their social support network.[8] They felt encouraged to remain with their abusers in order to maintain the network's positive image of their specific relationship:

> I can say what kinds of responses were least helpful. Those were the people who said 'You can't break up, you're my role models, you can't leave her!'

The position of lesbians in a heterosexist culture, in which all lesbian relationships are considered to be deviant or unacceptable, requires constant affirmation of the positive aspects of being lesbian. The concept of abuse by lesbians can be perceived as a threat to the positive images lesbian communities have struggled to affirm and celebrate.[9] Thus these women were caught between a heterosexist culture that did not affirm their sexuality, and a community that supported their sexuality but was not willing to accept the fact that they were abused.[10]

Thirdly, although on the whole the two African American women interviewed said little about negative responses from their support networks, one woman expressed surprise that I had been able to contact any other African American women willing to be interviewed, and explained why she thought that black women would be unlikely to discuss their experiences of abuse with a white researcher. Her commitment to the struggle against racial oppression inhibited her from identifying her partner as abusive. It is particularly painful, and against the American black culture's ethic of strength and survival, to speak out about being beaten by a black man.

Thus, the women did not always find affirmation of their experiences and achievements, even within communities that seemed to be united in a struggle against the values and beliefs of the dominant culture. The dynamics of power which encourage feminist, lesbian and black communities to create a strong defence against the oppression of white heterosexual male culture may also produce a type of single-mindedness within such communities. The self-hate and secrecy experienced by lesbians as a consequence of homophobia provide another weapon for abuse. Women abused by their lesbian partners find that often their communities struggle with accepting that abuse occurs, and the silence of abuse is even greater than in heterosexual culture. Thus abused lesbians have even fewer resources available from which to gain support. This is one way in which lesbian abuse is related to male control. The compulsory nature of heterosexuality which underlies abuse of heterosexual women in intimate relationships (see Chapter 2) also serves to silence lesbians and afford their partners greater control. Thus, lesbians struggle with the added dilemma of affirming their sexual identity in a homophobic society while also acknowledging within their own, sometimes resistant, communities that abuse occurs in lesbian relationships.

Thus, the cumulative effect of inaccurate media images, negative responses from family and friends and pressures from alternative support networks had enormous impact on formerly abused women. The women, who had fought to be free of abuse, found that their struggle was not recognized by others and, in some cases, was trivialized, devalued or misrepresented (although they also perceived that some people held the perspective that women who stay with abusers are 'deviant', which placed them in a contradictory double bind with respect to these attitudes). When their struggle to be free was not valued, the implication was that the women themselves were not valuable enough to warrant support for their freedom from abuse. Is this message not identical to the one enforced upon them by their abuser? In many ways, as I have noted throughout the section, women's encounters with those around them fed into the feelings they already held about having been abused. The social context – in terms of their personal community of friends, family and support networks as well as the representations they encounter from television and films – in which women seek to heal from abuse is, in general, unsupportive or detrimental to their efforts. In the next section, I will discuss one possible way in which this context might be challenged in order to create support for survivors of abuse.

The Need for a Language of Abuse

From women's discussions it became clear that there was a need for an appropriate language which would allow them to express the depth and quality of their experiences. When women tried to confront the perspectives or images held by others they found that, often, they simply did not know of appropriate words for their experiences. Thus, the silencing of women's experiences is reinforced by the lack of an appropriate language with which they can attempt to contradict predominant and misinformed images of 'battered women'. For example, one woman commented on the difficulty she had in describing to others the abusive nature of her partner's complete domination of her time, social contacts and life. She found that others continually redefined her descriptions in terms of normal tensions in relationships over negotiating the amount of time spent together or with friends:

> It's very hard to talk to other people about psychological abuse . . . Because everybody's lover is upset, everybody has time issues with their lover: 'How much time are you gonna spend with me?' Everybody has friend issues, a little competitiveness. To be able to talk about the magnitude of it and what the experience of it was like, is very hard.

This woman reveals the difficulty of speaking about the emotional experience of abuse. Yet, according to the comments of the women interviewed, talking about their experiences is particularly important because they had often kept the abuse silent for a long period. It became clear from the interviews that, in order to understand and process their experiences themselves, women need the opportunity to explain their perspectives to and test out their perceptions with others.

A vocabulary concerning women's experience of other kinds of violence, such as rape and incest, has begun to emerge. Use of the term 'survivor' is becoming more and more prevalent, thus putting a word to the skills developed and acts undertaken to cope with and heal physically and emotionally from their experiences. In terms of court or police treatment of women who have been raped, use of the term 'a second rape' conveys the trauma and emotional intensity experienced by women who are insensitively interrogated about the violence they have suffered. What is needed is a similar growth of vocabulary which addresses the experiences of formerly abused women. They are often seen as culpable for the abuse (see Chapter 1) and are judged in terms of why they did not leave an abuser more quickly than they did. A vocabulary along the lines of that introduced in Chapters 3 and 4 which addresses the personal impact and dynamics of abuse, as well as the long-term effects, needs to be adopted in order for women to combat such attitudes.

This need for a language is highly significant to the relation between feminist theories of woman abuse and those on the gender dynamics of power existing in Western society. Marilyn Frye, in discussion of what she titles *The Politics of Reality* (1983), asserts that 'definition is another face of power . . . The powerful normally determine what is said and sayable. When the powerful label something or dub it or baptize it, the thing becomes what they call it' (Frye, 1983: 105). The silencing of women's experience brought about by a dearth of language is part of the maintenance of women's power relation to men. In fact, as Frye points out, focus on the physical is characteristic of male definition. Thus the definition of 'battered women' as women who are physically attacked or injured without recognition of the deep destructive nature of emotional abuse, a definition which the women interviewed confronted continually, reflects the presence of male language in the popular definitions of women's experiences (Kelly, 1988b). When women can name their abuse, they not only further their opportunity for healing, but they also reclaim the power that has been used by others in creating false images or concepts about the nature of abuse. They reclaim the power to define and speak their reality.

The parallel, however, illuminates more than the relation between language and issues of empowerment confronted by formerly abused women. It also illuminates another tie between the dynamics of abuse and the specific cultural context in which it occurs. I see this relation from two angles of perspective. First, because the power to name is owned by men, women are rendered more vulnerable to abuse; and their process of healing from abuse is more complicated, as demonstrated in the discussions above, because they are denied access to this power. In this way, women's acknowledgement and freedom from abuse is not supported by their culture. A second angle from which to see this relation speaks to the wisdom that formerly abused women hold for understanding the way in which women seek to challenge their depowerment through language. Simply by speaking their stories, communicating the disparity between what they thought was important about their experiences and the language they had to describe them (and this communication took many different forms), women were working towards reclaiming the power denied them. This second angle, then, suggests that not only is abuse related in specific ways to the general power imbalances between men and women, but the voices of formerly abused women illustrate how women struggle to shift this general power imbalance.

To conclude, this chapter has considered how abuse and leaving an abuser impact the feelings of formerly abused women, and the ways in which representations of abuse on television, in films, in magazines and in newspapers were experienced as judgemental or were distorted as humorous or erotic. Moreover, the responses of friends, family and alternative support networks were largely described as judgemental or dismissive. In such circumstances, women find that the impact of abuse and leaving an abuser is compounded rather than alleviated. In fact, women who had been out of their relationships for over 15 years found that their experiences of abuse, as well as the impact of popular beliefs and media representations, were still issues in their lives, although with time the centrality of such issues diminished. In order to minimize or invert the effect of the images or views held by others, formerly abused women need to encounter attitudes which respect their wisdom about their own experiences and create a language which addresses the nature of these experiences. The way in which women attempted to challenge and overcome lasting legacies of abuse is the subject of Chapter 7, in which we will see how the long-term, negative impact of abuse and leaving an abuser can be transformed by women into an avenue for personal change and growth.

Notes

1 I use the term 'anxiety' in this analysis to reflect a dimension of the feeling of fear. Anxiety, in this sense, refers to the experience of persistent tension which, although it affects daily life, does not completely dominate perceptions or the ability to function, as does the overwhelming experience of terror.

2 Related to this issue is the discussion in Chapter 2 about the ethics of interviewing formerly abused women in the light of the fact that such interviews can have an intense impact on the women's lives.

3 Only one woman asserted that she did not experience anger towards her former partner. She had been out of her relationship for about three years. However, given that many women experienced their anger only after a year or two of independence or after counselling, it is possible that this woman may, at some point, experience this anger. It seems unlikely that one of 30 women would never experience anger when this emotion was so central to the experiences of others.

4 The majority of women commenting on helpful books were from the US. Such books as *The Battered Woman* (Walker, 1979a), *Battered Wives* (Martin, 1976), *Getting Free* (NiCarthy, 1986), *Rape in Marriage* (Russell, 1982) and *Naming the Violence* (Lobel, 1986) were all mentioned as being helpful, suggesting that there is some appropriate information available, at least in the US.

5 Hoff researched the attitudes of informal support networks including families and friends, for nine formerly abused women in the US. She found that not all family members were indifferent to the circumstances of battered women; some were genuinely dismayed but were unable to help women for complex reasons. Moreover, service organizations and agencies, with the exception of refuges, on the whole offered indifferent or negative responses to women both when they were in relationships with abusers and once they had left. She demonstrated that agencies such as housing authorities often took a 'victim-blaming' stance, and thus were seen as not particularly helpful to the women. This survey of network responses and values corresponds with the description women in this study gave of the responses offered by many family members, friends and services organizations (Hoff, 1990).

6 The Native American and Hispanic women interviewed felt that their ethnicity had little effect on their experiences. However, other researchers have indicated that, for some abused women of colour, ethnicity and race have an impact on their experiences (Center for the Prevention of Sexual and Domestic Violence, 1986).

7 Of the two women from lesbian relationships, one had been out of her relationship for two years and the other for three years at the time of the interviews. Thus, although there has been some change in the acknowledgement of abuse in lesbian relationships (Hart, 1986; 1988; Kelly et al., 1989; Kelly, 1991; Lobel, 1986), the experiences related here can be taken to be fairly recent within this period of change.

8 Although there is some overlap between the people in each of these types of group, lesbian support networks differ in that they are united in their struggle against heterosexism rather than violence against women in particular. As a result, they form a specific network in which lesbians may express their feelings about their relationships with women and their lives more freely and openly, without the homophobic attitudes they might confront from other groups. So, lesbians can be especially reliant on lesbian support networks for positive affirmation of their lifestyles and sexual identity.

9 In fact, there is a close relationship between heterosexism and the response of lesbian support networks to women abused by lesbian partners. The former requires the establishment and unification of alternative support networks in order for lesbians to feel affirmed and positive about their sexualities and lifestyles. Yet, because the social pressure to be in a heterosexual partnerhsip is extreme, lesbian communities consistently struggle to affirm relationships with women (Benowitz, 1986; Hammond, 1986). Often the struggle to affirm healthy and positive relationships between women blinds a support network to the possibility that abuse can occur (Edgington, 1988; Hammond, 1986; Hart, 1986; 1988; KALX Radio, 1985). The heterosexism of society at large, then, places women who are abused within lesbian relationships in a particularly vulnerable position.

10 Although these women spoke of their experiences in the US, the issue of lesbian abuse in Britain has just begun to surface (Kelly et al., 1989; Kelly, 1991). The fact that I was unable to contact any women for interview illustrates how deeply lesbian abuse is silenced in Britain and suggests that similar circumstances might also be faced by abused lesbians in this country.

7

Victims and Survivors: Concepts and Issues
Central to Women's Action for Change

I think that it made me feel like a victim and see my attempts at whatever as just another way to become victimized and it was really hard to get past that . . . But I knew that I just had to change the way I was dealing with things because I just couldn't live like that anymore. I felt so totally vulnerable because I never had any limits. It *had* to be that way because I didn't have any in-betweens. And I didn't know how to say *no* to people that *needed* me . . . It was a big big change but it was something I just had to do, I *knew* it. I just knew I could not go on living and always end up being the loser, being the person who got stomped on . . . I think for a long time it was some kind of merit of honour that I could absorb all that pain and still go on, that somehow that was a 'good' thing and *finally* I just said I *can't* do that.

Seeing the possibility for change, visualizing a different kind of behaviour from that required to cope with an abusive relationship, setting the limits of what one will accept and will not accept: these are hurdles which women describe over and over again. The women interviewed have survived and escaped abuse. But they then faced a process of assessing their own behaviour, discovering and analysing the ways in which they had been forced to adopt depowered behaviour and self-perspectives as a result of the unbalanced power dynamics created by their partners' abuse. Part of the way in which women survived abuse itself was to adapt their behaviour and perceptions to fit the circumstances in which they lived. For example, if women did not see any avenue of escape from an abusive relationship, some adopted the survival tactic of not questioning or challenging the emotional and physical attacks perpetuated by their abusers.[1] This type of adaptation was functional until a way to end the relationship was discovered. In this sense 'acceptance' of abuse, which took the form of not challenging or not speaking to others about the abuse, was part of the way women adapted to extremely painful and threatening circumstances. It was a way they sought to minimize emotional and physical injury within the relationship. This type of behaviour is generally what feminists refer to as 'survival skills', which allow women to continue living and functioning in the face of abuse (Barry, 1979; Hoff, 1990; Kelly, 1988b, Stanko, 1985).

Yet the term 'survivors' has also been loosely applied by feminists to women who have freed themselves of abuse and in the context of the struggles they face at this time (Hoff, 1990; Stanko, 1985). This differentiation in terminology which exists in the literature was more vividly present in the interviews I conducted. Once women had freed themselves from the abuse of their former partners, they began to question and change their behaviour and perceptions. With regard to this process of personal change, women expressed their thoughts and experiences in terms such as 'victim' and 'survivor'. It became apparent that there are various meanings attached to these terms by the women in applying them to their own experiences. Moreover, *both* terms were personally useful to the women interviewed in understanding what has happened to them.

An Analysis of the Concept 'Victimization'

Central to a discussion of women's retrospective assessments of personal change is an understanding of the word 'victim'. The word 'victim' is used both in theoretical analyses of abuse against women as a social phenomenon, and in the way in which individual abused women understand themselves, and in each use the meaning is extremely different. When I began this study I was, and I still am, convinced of the need for a term such as 'survivor', which describes the kind of active, positive action women take to continue functioning within an abusive relationship, or to free themselves from abuse. The word 'survivor', used instead of 'victim', is useful in conveying that abused and formerly abused women are not passive in their experience of abuse, and affirms the strength and skills women develop to survive abuse. Such skills and strengths were described in Chapter 4 in terms of how women coped with abuse and eventually shifted the power imbalance created by their partners. Moreover, from a theoretical perspective, assigning the status of 'victim' to women who have suffered violence skews the focus of analysis away from the behaviour of those who enact violence and towards the behaviour of those who suffer from it (Barry, 1979; Stanko, 1985).[2] In this way, use of the word 'victim' can be extremely misleading and can place responsibility for violence on the women who are attacked.

However, from listening to the descriptions of the way in which women heal and reclaim the power they hold over their lives, it became clear that there were two ways in which the term 'victim' was useful. Both of these suggest that women's use of the term represents to them the process by which their personal power was eroded. Thus the term 'victim', which feminists have argued negatively labels abused women, is often used by women themselves to name the process of victimization enacted by their abusers. First, there was a high degree of personal value in words which described the position of not being allowed by their partners to control their lives. The word 'victim' was used to convey the feeling of losing control over one's life which occurred as abusers increased their control within the relationships. In this context, the term 'victimization' has a fairly basic definition. For the women interviewed it meant simply that they were rendered unable to change the circumstances in which abuse occurred. This was so when women were physically overpowered or financially deprived, such that they could not leave their partners, as well as when abuse prevented them from drawing upon their own personal resources, as described in Chapter 4.

Secondly, once women progressed outward along the spiral of relationship dynamics and eventually left their abusers, they became aware of some of the behaviour which they were required to adopt in order to cope with abuse and which was part of the depowered position forced upon them by their partners. From this *retrospective* viewpoint, the concept of victimization was useful in a different way. It named the depowering perspectives and behaviours they developed as a response to abuse, but which, once out of their relationships, they had the freedom to change for their own empowerment. Thus, women used words such as 'victim' and 'martyr' to help illuminate the kinds of perspectives they held about themselves as a result of abuse, which persisted after the relationship ended and which they could actively reject or continue to hold. Moreover, their use of these words illustrated the degree to which they had changed their perspectives, and helped to punctuate their disbelief at their former feelings of worth-lessness and experience of victimization:

> I'm not a martyr anymore, I was such a martyr it was unbelievable, it was sickening . . . when I think about it now, like I used to get really upset and hurt and think nobody cares or nothin'. I put myself down in that position. I laid myself down as the victim. So long as I was layin' myself down as a doormat, people are gonna walk across and I had absolutely no right to complain about it.

> I felt a victim for a long while but now I'm in control of my own life . . . I think it took time . . . I think certain things had to happen for me to come to this point . . . but I'm healthier today, and I'm happier, feel a lot better about myself.

These women use the terms 'victim' and 'martyr' to name the depowered behaviours their partners' abuse required they adopt and the process of victimization enacted by their abusers. By naming them women can then use these names as tools in their movement toward more empowered ways of being, once they are free from abuse.

I have attempted to separate women's common sense use of the term 'victim' in reference to women's processes of personal change from explanations of abuse in which looking at the 'victim' behaviour of formerly abused women is labelling and excludes the agency of the abuser. This latter approach, as described in Chapter 1, removes focus from the social conditions which support abuse and from the actual responsibility of the abuser for his or her actions.

Survival

The term that has been used by feminists as a replacement for the common use of 'victim' is 'survivor'. This term also had significant meaning for formerly abused women, but its use does not preclude the usefulness of the terms 'victim' or 'victimization' described above. Again in understanding the experiences of women described to me, words that denote process rather than serve as labels are most useful. Hence I will use the word 'survival' rather than 'survivor'. This is a translation of women's use of the term 'survivor' which, like their use of 'victim', usually referred to a process. 'Survival' for formerly abused women refers to action taken first to minimize the frequency of occurrence and degree of abuse (Barry, 1979; Hoff, 1990; Stanko, 1985), and second to reverse or transform its effect.[3] Unlike victimization, in which the agent is the abuser, the agent of survival is the abused woman. Thus, women are often simultaneously victimized and actively surviving (Hooper, 1991).

For example, a woman who was physically or verbally attacked by her partner because, according to her abuser, she had not put dinner on the table by a specific time, was victimized in the basic definition of the word. She was being abused. However, she was also coping with this abuse by trying to avoid any circumstances which might aggravate future attacks, i.e. she subsequently placed high priority on getting dinner on the table. She was working to survive because she acted to minimize the degree or frequency with which attacks occurred. Whether her efforts were successful or not in avoiding attack – and, for most, such tactics were useful only in prolonging the onset of attacks if they had any effect at all – she was actively involved in minimizing the abuse in any possible way. Thus the words 'victimization' and 'survival', for formerly abused women, were not mutually exclusive. Rather, they refer to two processes of women's experiences which have different agents for their enactment. What makes abuse so insidious and difficult to cope with is that the very acts of survival described here can be coopted by abusers into the process of victimization. While she watches the clock and times her cooking to meet her partner's schedule, her attention is increasingly monopolized. Although she may avert an imminent attack, she is being emotionally abused and victimized because her attention is becoming focused predominantly or entirely on her partner's needs. This is why the web of abuse is so effective: surviving physical abuse rendered this woman more vulnerable to control through emotional abuse. Thus, survival of both physical and emotional abuse requires a shift in power dynamics as described in Chapter 4, which allows women to leave their partners.

In this chapter I will focus primarily on a second meaning of survival: how women transform the impact of abuse after the relationships have ended. Feminist analysis has looked at this kind of survival in the context of women's experiences of rape and, recently, has begun to extend this to the experiences of formerly abused women (Kelly, 1988b).

Survival is a process. It is a gradual movement through dimensions of increasing empowerment[4] borne out of the experiences of abuse. As women increasingly saw their behaviour as once essential to coping with abuse but now an impediment to their own freedom and control over their lives, they moved through a process of survival. One formerly abused woman who was currently a counsellor and had worked with survivors of abuse explained:

> It's real important that people working with women who are *survivors*, allow them to take control and recognize, maybe destructive behaviour patterns – but even the words 'destructive behaviour patterns' is scary. The idea is that what they've learned is ways that they have learned to stay alive . . . and now they're not working anymore and things are falling apart. And because those patterns and because those tools that you used to have are no longer . . . fixing the way you're living, you need to learn new ways. And that's a *process* and that's *slow*.

The freedom from physical and emotional abuse allowed for seeing new possibilities of being, understanding and exploring one's own needs and self. Ultimately, survival is the active use of this freedom to minimize, reverse or transform negative, depowering experiences into wisdom and skills for empowerment.

Yet, there were many dimensions of survival enacted by women after they had left their partners. From the experiences of the women interviewed, three were identified: addressing, exploring and fulfilling one's needs; asserting one's needs in relationships with others; and acting for change for abused women in general. I will now address each in turn, focusing on aspects of survival experienced once relationships with abusers have ended. These dimensions of survival may be seen as an extension of outward movement along the spiral. I will return to this concept later, but I offer it here as an additional context in which to understand the following discussion.

*Dimension One: Addressing, Exploring and Fulfilling One's
Own Needs*

Dimension one is a transformation of the behaviour adopted to cope
with abuse in which the women became focused on the needs and
wishes of their abusers. In leaving their partners they had begun to
become aware of their own needs as described in Chapter 4. Yet, they
still faced the enormous task of discovering the ways in which they
habitually ignored many of their own wants and desires and of
exploring how they, themselves, might fulfil these. They moved
forward in this process both by trying out new ways of living and by
seeking the aid of people who supported this.

Once women were out of their relationships with abusers and
had settled into a permanent home – i.e. somewhere where they
would be living for more than a few weeks or months – they continued the process of exploring their needs and wishes that they
had already begun in leaving their partners. Central to the
continuation of this process was the knowledge that they had the
increased control over their own time and space that comes with
finding permanent homes. This increase in freedom allowed women to
explore much more deeply and minutely their own needs. They
described this emerging sense of identity and self-esteem as one of the
most dramatic and liberating changes that occurred after leaving their
partners:

> So I decided to take a few months out, no work, no cleanin', no anything . . .
> it's enabled me to clear things out of the way a bit and come to some
> decisions for *me*. Which has been *really*, it's been really exciting. It *really is*
> exciting to realize all of a sudden it *is* just *me*. I don't have to think about *him*
> or his reactions . . . I've really thought more deeply than I ever have before.
> And I realize just how much I, the whole of my life has been coloured by
> what other people's expectations, or the fear of other people's reactions to
> what I decided to do.

Similarly, women spoke of a gradual realization of their own needs and
of action which would fulfil those needs. What they discovered varied
enormously. One-fifth of the women were returning to college and
furthering their education or taking part in a careers advisory course to
identify their area of desired employment. Most women spoke of their
skills in developing, decorating and DIY for their own homes, in order
to create an environment which suited their individual tastes and
requirements. This fulfilled women's need for a sense of competence,
for creativity and for exploring their tastes. Others developed a musical
skill or made radical changes in dress and hair to express their
creativity and individuality. Women also made more time simply to
relax and enjoy themselves:

> Friday nights is my night. I'll take a bath. I'll take an hour, hour and a half, just turn the radio on, lay in there. And the kid'll try 'Can I come in?' and I say 'No, you go over there, this is my time, this is my time.'

Finally, just over one-tenth of the women described a period of 'wildness', either referring to exploring their sexual freedom or testing out new freedoms through the use of drugs or alcohol:

> I had a lot of little affairs and I was doing a lot of drinking and drugs and all kinds of stuff, after I got loose, so to speak. So it wasn't an instant 'know thyself' sort of thing . . . I think it was being out of control a little bit . . . I just had no responsibility and I really enjoyed it.

For all of these women, however, after a few months or just over a year of this period, they returned to a lifestyle that they saw as less 'wild'. In retrospect, women spoke of how such 'wildness' not only served to extend their sense of freedom, but also numbed the pain of coping with emerging feelings about having been abused. So, although they eventually wanted to minimize the latter consequence, they also gained from these periods a sense of their own freedom to choose the type of lifestyles they wanted.

By finding the time and space to focus on their current lifestyles, then, women made numerous changes in their lives, from the subtle taking of two hours a week for a special bath to returning to college. Each of these changes was related to women's survival because it marked their deepening sensitivity to, respect for and willingness to act upon their own wants and desires. This was precisely what women lost in response to being abused. So, the process of rebuilding their responses to their own needs was central to reversing the impact of abuse.

In addition to acting on their own insights, women sought the support of one or a few individuals who could encourage and accompany them in this process. Despite the negative responses from many friends and family members, each woman usually had one or two people in her life who were open to hearing and supporting her. Women spoke of seeking the help of friends, refuge staff, single-parent family agencies and counsellors to help them reverse the impact of abuse and move on to fulfilling lifestyles.

One of the few differences in the experiences of US and British women is that women from the States had available to them, and three-fourths used, counselling or therapy to facilitate this change. Women from the US either sought it from private therapists or received subsidized counselling from organizations for abused women.[5] In contrast, only one British woman sought counselling from a professional. In general, British women tended to look to counsellors to help with problems within the relationship, but did not feel that counselling services were appropriate for the emotional crises they faced after leaving their partners. This contrasts with British women's use of medical practitioners, to whom some went with emotional and personal issues, as described in Chapter 5. Both British and US women received informal counselling from refuge staff, agencies for single parents or friends. Women described how the support from these sources offered them some of the skills used in counselling such as respectful listening.

Thus, both British and US formerly abused women sought to clarify their perceptions and to gain support for personal change from others. One woman described the benefits from this. Although her experience was with a professional counsellor, it reflects the kinds of support US and British women sought in formal or informal counselling:

> I wouldn't be where I was if I didn't have therapy ... By being in a situation where you get a *totally* objective viewpoint, you don't feel like it's a judgement because he backs it up with facts and experience – clarity, you just get clarity in therapy.

In discovering people willing to offer objective and respectful perspectives on their experiences, the women interviewed found environments in which they could explore the connections between abuse and their current ways of living, and expose the ways in which they were ignoring their own wants and desires with respect to their lives.[6]

Dimension Two: Asserting Self and Personal Needs in Relationships with Others

When women began to acknowledge and act to fulfil their own wishes about how they wanted their lives to be, they were faced with how this change affected their relationships with others. This was a second dimension of survival because women actually began to assert the importance of their own wishes within relationships. Because it was in a relationship that they had been denied the importance of their needs, this practice began to reverse the impact of abuse within the circumstances similar to those in which it was enacted. Women spoke of becoming more assertive within a variety of relationships: intimate; with family; with friends or colleagues; and with their children.

Intimate Relationships   One-third of the women, at the time of interview, were or had been involved with intimate partners since the ending of their relationships with abusers. They described the struggles they faced in not bringing the devaluation of their own needs, learned from their abusers, into their new relationships. These women asserted their needs within the intimate relationships in a number of ways.

First, half of these women explained how they required sufficient time and space to maintain lives independently from their new relationships. They said that they enjoyed living on their own rather than moving in with their partners and clearly explained to their partners that they had no present intention of living with them. All of them also described taking more time to develop aspects of themselves, emphasizing the importance of this need when new partners expressed a desire to spend more time together. For example, one woman continually asserted to her new partner, who was putting her under pressure to spend more time together, that she needed specific parts of the day to work on her writing – an important aspect of self-expression and personal progress as a professional author – as well as time every day to herself. Regardless of the wants of her new partner, she acknowledged that this time was critically important to her as an individual and was not willing to compromise on the issue of time spent together. She also explained the importance of this wish for time in terms of her past experience of abuse. Eventually her new partner became accepting of her wishes and both continued to enjoy the relationship.

Secondly, women described how they no longer accepted any behaviour which they felt was disrespectful of those wants. For example, one woman explained that her new partner phoned her and told her he was on his way over, rather than asking her if he could come. His total disregard for her plans and wishes was unacceptable and she expressed her anger on his arrival, letting him know that if he continued to treat her in such a way she would no longer want to continue the relationship.

Finally, all of these women were specific about their wish for non-aggressive behaviour. If their new partners expressed any violence or aggression in anger, then they made it clear that this was not acceptable. For most, this assertion was accompanied by an explanation of why they were particularly sensitive to aggression. For these women, such self-disclosure meant that it was even more important for their new partners to respect their wishes, simply because these partners knew why such respect was necessary. For others, fear that their past experiences of abuse would be used against them kept them silent about why any form of aggression was unacceptable. NiCarthy, in her work with formerly abused women, notes that this fear can be well founded and suggests that women not tell new partners about their past experiences of abuse (NiCarthy, 1986). Thus women often told of times when they confronted their partner's aggression in play or in anger, re-emphasizing that they would not accept such behaviour within their relationships.

All three examples of women's assertion of their wants and desires with intimate partners demonstrate how women became actively involved in preventing involvement with another abuser. Similarly, their interactions with others reflected their growing sense of self-respect and of knowledge about their own wishes.

Family   Women also described how their relationships with family changed. Obviously, these relationships had existed for a long time, both before and during the periods in which women were abused. Thus the assertions women made within their families challenged long-term, mutually accepted ways of behaving together. These were critical to women's process of change and survival because they marked the courage and skill to assert themselves even in long-standing relationships.[7]

With regard to family, women spoke primarily of their mothers. Central to asserting their own needs was communicating to their mothers that they wanted the freedom to live their lives without criticism or intervention. So, for example, one woman who was very close to her mother normally saw her at least once a week and had spoken with her about her experience of leaving her partner. Yet, over time, it became clear that her mother, in trying to support her through the ending of the relationship, was intervening too much in her life – suggesting how she could raise the children, that she shouldn't live alone, etc. Thus, although she had never before challenged her mother's overprotectiveness and suggestions, she found that, as she became more aware of her own wishes concerning her lifestyle, her mother's intervention felt like an intrusion, regardless of her good intent. Eventually she confronted her mother, explaining that she intended to raise her children, remain single, and create the kind of life she wanted, regardless of the misgivings voiced by her mother. Over time, her mother came to accept this and they still continued to see each other regularly. In asserting herself, then, she challenged the very structure of their relationship and forged within it more respect for her own wants. Her experience is not unique. One-third of the women described similar interactions, particularly with their mothers but also with fathers and siblings, in which they re-formed the relationships to accommodate a deeper respect for their own wishes and desires.

Friends and Colleagues   Likewise, with friends and colleagues, women found that they changed relationships by asserting themselves. Women's descriptions revealed how they became increasingly clear and active about establishing with others what type of behaviour they would and would not accept. They also became clear about how they wanted to invest themselves in friendships and relationships. In this way they actively supported the importance of their own wants concerning the nature of their friendships and shifted their attention away from the wishes of others, a focus deeply enforced within the abusive relationship:

> And I often say to other people that I have to do what's best for *me*. And that was a statement that I didn't ever make before, *ever ever*. I never said I had to do what's best for me cause that sounded just so terribly selfish. But *now, reality* is I *have* to do what's best for me.

> I carry myself differently, I hold my head up, I'm more assertive. I've noticed even in my work life if someone does something I don't feel is right I speak up. And just this whole thing has taught me that I don't have to take it . . . I've learned that when you speak up and stand up for yourself, people respect you more.

Thus relationships with friends and colleagues also underwent major transformations as women asserted their wishes with the confidence that they were as important as those of others.

Children   A final type of relationship which women transformed was that with their children. This was especially complex because women were aware of both their own wants as well as the demands of their children. Particularly because some of the children had suffered emotionally or physically from the abuse enacted by the former partners and were experiencing the conflict that comes from separation of parents, women were extremely aware and concerned that their children's well-being should not suffer owing to any other circumstances. All the women with children spoke of periods in which their children were extremely distressed by the abuse that had occurred and/ or by the separation of their parents. Having left a relationship, partly in order to meet the needs of their children, and because they were faced with raising children who had been affected both by the relationship and by the separation, women found the assertion of their own wants in their relationships with children painful and complicated.

Many women asserted their needs by taking time away from their children for themselves. The time they did spend with them was more focused on the children's needs and development. This in effect balanced the two needs: time for women to enjoy themselves, and the parental attention required by the children.

However, not all balancing between a woman's needs and those of her children was satisfactory. Often women were forced to choose between resolutions to conflicts of needs which were all extremely painful:

> When I started doing things it bothered [my daughter], she liked me always being at home. And I think for my own emotional health it's important for me to do the things that I'm doing. And I thought about cutting back on

those things for her. And I realized that I would be doing the same things I had done in the past which is play the role of a martyr. And I decided that, if it's not healthy for *me*, then it's not healthy for her to see me do it. And it was really hard for me because I knew she was gonna leave . . . The results have been really painful and I don't know what will happen in the long run. But I don't think I could live with myself if I were doing what she wanted me to do, and it's not what I want.

This woman, then, decided that being a positive role model required that she take her own wants seriously and weigh them carefully with the demands of her children. This consideration led to a radical decision about the involvement of the child's father, as her daughter decided that she would prefer to live with her father rather than her mother, and about how to be an effective mother. Clearly, assertion of her own wishes, even when combined with meeting the long-term needs of her child, necessitated an emotionally courageous act and resulted in the deeply painful loss of living with her daughter.

Thus when women asserted their own needs within their relationships with children they were faced with a balancing act. The resolutions reached which respect the needs of both can necessitate radical changes in the relationships and in women's approaches to mothering.

In summary, the type of damage wrought by emotional abuse, and reinforced by physical abuse, in which women's respect for their own wants and desires was eroded or destroyed, was central to the experiences of abused women. So, reversing this damage by drawing clear lines about the extent to which others could encroach upon their rights, freedom and wishes was extremely important to formerly abused women and was enforced throughout their relationships. Within this dimension, survival consisted of reversing the denial of personal needs and wants demanded by abusers through asserting them in relationships with others. In this way, women created for themselves healthier relationships in which their wishes and wants were not as likely to be ignored, either by themselves or by others.

Dimension Three: Effecting Change for Abused Women

A third and final dimension of survival comprised women's action for broad social change which would relieve the circumstances confronting those who leave abusive partners. A majority of women interviewed had had contact with empowerment-oriented agencies or perspectives. Thus this dimension of survival is probably least likely to be generalizable to the experience of all formerly abused women. Yet, from my work in the movement against woman abuse it has become clear to me that although not all formerly abused women act for change, many of the women who contribute strength and insight to the movement for change draw from their various experiences of victimization. Thus the topic of this section is important because it underlies a core element of change for formerly abused women and illustrates the dimensions to which survival can extend. It also expands the idea of women's paths of change, which has often been described as individual and personal change (Mann, 1987), to include political action which challenges the social system that acts against abused women. For these reasons, I choose to focus at length on the topic of creating broad change, not because I am implying that all formerly abused women choose to enact their survival along this dimension.

As described in Chapters 5 and 6, the women confronted problems with organizations and state institutions, as well as inappropriate images in the media and in the beliefs and attitudes of those around them. All of these problems were part of what women described as circumstances which supported abuse but which lay outside the dynamics of their relationships. Thus in minimizing, reversing and transforming the impact of abuse, some women sought to change the circumstances which they felt impeded or complicated their independence from their abusers, and to contribute to the support of abused women in general. In doing so, they aimed to help reduce the number of women who were in or might enter abusive relationships, and to transform the effect of abuse on themselves by turning the lessons they had learned into wisdom for social change. That this was important to women in their process of survival was demonstrated by two themes in the interviews.

First, nearly all the women expressed their views about the ways in which the general problem of woman abuse was part of a social problem, rather than an individual, personal problem. This was evident when they were asked about what kinds of changes needed to be made to reduce women's likelihood of being abused. Women spoke of social change: changes in the beliefs held about women, the opportunities open to them, the amount of information available to women, the way men are socialized, and the degree of seriousness with which society regards violence against and abuse of women. Although personal change was of great importance to individual women in their processes of healing and empowerment, they expressed the view that the changes necessary to end abuse in general had to do with social change, not personal changes in individual women.

To this end, women expressed their desires to contribute their efforts to social change. This is the second theme. For example, one woman explained her motivation to work in a refuge for abused women:

> Being able to educate women that they're not second to men and that we can change the system, and that is a long process . . . we may not see all the changes here in our lifetime, but we can create change and pass it on to our

kids, our male and female children and *they* can run with it. And some of them will get it and some of them won't and, hopefully, they'll just grow.

Her enthusiasm for long-term social change was echoed in the efforts of others and expressed how important it was for many women interviewed to see that they contributed to ending the circumstances which supported their own abuse. As will be addressed in the following section, the specific ways in which women acted for change varied, but the will and enthusiasm behind their actions was typified by the passage above.

In the following sections I will take a closer look at this last level of survival. This will include both how women act for social change and the specific ways in which their actions affect their personal processes of survival.

Action for Social Change The ways in which the women worked towards change for abused women differed greatly. Three kinds of action described in the interviews were: working for organizations which aid abused women; offering support to friends who were abused; and contributing to public knowledge about abuse or serving as a role model for others by voicing personal experience. All these types of action were similar in that motivation for them lay in changing the circumstances, external to abusive relationships, which they felt had affected their experiences. Moreover, all provided a service to abused women which was helpful to the process of leaving abusive partners.

One-third of the women interviewed engaged in employment or volunteer work which involved some aspect of providing support, aid and information to abused women. These women worked at refuges or shelters or provided counselling or support groups for abused women. A further fifth planned or seriously considered getting involved in this type of aid sometime in the future, or contributed to the running of such organizations by making donations, by doing voluntary office work or by providing support for organization workers such as child care. In doing so, they added to the availability of aid for abused women which offered help with short-term housing, advice about obtaining finances and long-term housing, counselling and support.

In addition, one-half of the women described situations where they helped abused women on a one-to-one basis. This included providing support for and commitment to friends who were being abused. These women were able to offer empathy, experience and patience to women who suffered from the low self-esteem and inability to perceive options for change that are part of the mechanisms of abuse created by partners. Specifically, women spoke of listening to friends in a non-judgemental manner, providing physical help when their friends decided to leave partners, and simply supporting friends in their process of leaving and surviving abuse, regardless of the length of time this process might take:

> Actually my best friend is in a situation that – although it is not life threatening . . . it's emotionally abusive. And we talk several times a week about it. I guess really for the last year she's been thinking about leaving. And all I feel I can do for her is share my own experiences and feelings.

In this way, the women interviewed provided another source of support that, on the whole, they felt had been lacking in their own experiences of leaving their partners. They offered to others empathy and patience in contrast to the many negative types of responses they felt they had often experienced themselves.

Finally, women contributed to public understanding of abuse by voicing their experiences. The most striking example comes from this research project itself. Women expressed that one of their major motivations for contacting me and agreeing to be interviewed was to provide information and insight which might help other women who are abused. Women spoke of overcoming their fears about speaking to me of the past because they knew their voices could help others.

> One part of you's sayin' 'Don't do it' another part's sayin' 'Well why not?, cause people *have* to know these things happen.'

In speaking out about their experiences, then, women wanted to be involved actively in creating a society in which abuse was taken seriously and the needs of the abused women could be met. Particularly by speaking about their experience, they moved towards challenging the stereotypes which they saw to be held about abused women, creating a more accurate image of the experience of being abused and leaving an abuser, and serving as role models for women struggling with abuse (Kelly, 1988b).

The Effect of Combining Personal Change with Action for Social Change   The dimension of survival which is action taken to minimize, reverse and transform the impact of abuse is sometimes double edged. Women must face the pain of their experiences of abuse over and over again in order to effectively engage with and respectfully support women in similar circumstances or to speak about their experiences. In this section, then, I will show how survival was related to women's action for social change as well as describe the challenges they faced in acting in this dimension.

First, working with abused women validated for them that they had made personal change. By being faced with the early steps of leaving an abuser, women remembered the struggles they had overcome. The women gained support from this clear indication of the degree to which they had succeeded in their survival. This, in turn, encouraged them to continue the process:

> I think giving support to other women is helpful. I think that working with other women and watching them go through different stages of their crisis and moving forward helps reinforce your own going forward ... I think it's helped me forgive myself a lot, and really *really* recognize that it's not me. It helps me stay focused.

Secondly, working with abused or formerly abused women also offered the women interviewed an opportunity for the powerful trans-formation of their experiences with abuse into wisdom and skill. Because these women had been through the process of leaving, they knew what women were experiencing first hand. Consequently, they felt they were able to lend informed, empathetic and respectful support and advice borne from personal experience when other women suffered from low self-esteem or confused identity. However, tasks through which they transformed their experiences into wisdom and skill also required that they remain in touch with the pain they had experienced. Being faced with the experiences of other women brought to the surface intense feelings about their own. Intense contact with abused women in crisis, for example, touched on many personal issues for the women providing support:

> That's the one thing about the shelter, about it being painful, is the people stir up *so* much in you and you can't shelve it, it'd be difficult to do that. You have to do something with that internally. And hopefully it'll have some effect on the system.

This woman remarked on the fine line between using personal insight to increase the effectiveness of her work with abused women and being overwhelmed by the intensity of her own emotions. Again she stressed that, in order to achieve the former and thus move forward in her own process of growth and change, support and the opportunity to address personal pain were crucial. In her case, this support was provided by a refuge counsellor who offered ongoing therapy to refuge residents, a status this particular woman had held previously.

The process of survival within this dimension, then, was not one of 'forgetting' the past or 'leaving the past behind' but one of remember-ing, using and transforming the past to build upon a more empowered self, a fulfilled life and a changed society.

In conclusion we can see that, after leaving their abusers, women undergo a process of survival which spans three dimensions and which may continue for years. This extends the current feminist use of the term 'survivor' which, when applied to abused women, commonly refers to their coping strategies within their relationships. Within this process, it was clear that women found the concepts of 'victimization' and 'survival' equally important: the former in naming the ways in which their abusers coerced them into changing their behaviours and perspectives, and the latter in naming how they acted to change this effect. Each has its place in women's descriptions and, as such, each is an important part of the vocabulary used by women to understand their processes of personal change and healing.

Notes

1 By speaking of how women do not question their partners' behaviour I am referring to the kinds of dynamics discussed in the inward cycle of Chapter 4. For example, as a woman feels less and less confident about her own perceptions of herself and the relationship, the less she feels voicing these perceptions is worth the risk of challenging an abusive partner. Paradoxically, she is attempting to minimize the abuse she is experiencing by silencing herself, while this same action is contributing to her loss of power in the relationship. It is both an action of survival and a part of the dynamics in which she loses control over her life.

2 Furthermore, feminists have revealed how use of the word 'victim', rather than 'survivor', within analyses of why abuse occurs, implies that the behaviour of women has a contributing causal role in the problem of abuse. Elizabeth Stanko describes this phenomenon:

> In applying the word 'victim', one implicitly separates victim from non-victim. Accordingly, victim characteristics are then explored by theorists for their contribution to patterns of criminal behaviour. Women – as a special group – are considered worthy of study; men are not . . . Suspicions regarding a 'victim's' behaviour – what led the man to attack the woman? – have foundations in the assumptions about typical and aberrant male behaviour. A woman 'victim' is thus seen as separate from women who are not victims of male violence. (1985: 13–14)

3 Much of the literature on incest refers to adult 'survivors' of incest. In this literature, 'survival skills' are generally taken to refer to 'abused children's attempts to deal with a situation they are powerless to change' (Women's Research Centre, 1989: 134) and include a variety of coping strategies (Kenney, 1989). However, the term has begun to broaden in its use such that, in some of the literature, 'survivors' and 'survival' are written about in the context of how women cope with or heal from incest once the abuse has stopped (Courtois, 1988; Stanko, 1985; Women's Research Centre, 1989). The term 'survivors' has also become associated with the movement to provide services for women who have experienced incest to protest court findings or media representations which unfairly or prejudicially approach the issue of incest, such as the work of Incest Survivors Campaign in Britain (Nelson, 1987). My use of the term reflects this transition in the literature. Rather than as a name for the coping mechanisms adopted by abused women, I use 'survival' to describe the transitions formerly abused women make in integrating their experiences with abuse into their lives as they progress towards healed lifestyles and self-perspectives.

4 In this book, 'empowerment' is used to refer to the process by which women gained increasing control over their lives and confidence in their ability to cope with problems and obstacles that arose. It is related to the discussion of power in Chapter 4 in that empowerment is the use of personal resources to establish increased control and influence over one's own life. This differs slightly from the use of the term 'power', which

refers to the personal resources brought to bear on influencing one's own or another's life.

5 Interviews with US women differed from those with British women because the former commonly had a larger vocabulary and conceptual framework, derived from the field of counselling and therapy, which they used in describing their experiences of personal change. For example, they used terms such as 'merger' to describe what happens when a person's individual identity becomes indistinct from the identity of their partner and the way the couple interacts within the relationship. US women also spoke of 'setting boundaries' when speaking of asserting how much of themselves they were willing to compromise in relationships with others. The concepts underlying these terms were not specific to US women who had been to therapists, however. The two above concepts were described by other US and British women in phrases such as 'losing oneself' or 'not letting people get away with that any more', respectively. So, the experiences of personal change were not qualitatively different. However, the US women who had been to therapy seemed more confident in describing their emotional experiences because they had access to well defined terminology with which they felt comfortable. I have already addressed the issue of appropriate language in terms of women's description of abuse (earlier in this chapter). It is clear that formal counselling or therapy can introduce women to terms which help them name and thus formally acknowledge some aspects of their experiences and, in this way, helps meet the needs of formerly abused women.

6 For women who had been abused either in previous relationships or as children, exploring these past experiences was central to healing from the more current abuse within this dimension of survival. These women explained again and again how they saw similarities between their past and more recent experiences and how change required an understanding of all the abuse they had suffered. However, it is important to note that the issue of women's previous experiences with abuse is addressed in terms of their healing process, not, as in some literature (see Chapter 1), in relation to a predisposition to entering abusive relationships. Not all the women interviewed had been abused previously to the relationships we discussed. Thus, I am not suggesting a link between past abuse and women who are again abused by partners.

7 Lerner (1990) asserts, from her therapeutic work, that such acts, in which women confront family members about behaviour which in the past has been implicitly accepted, is experienced by them as extremely risky and thus requires an immense courage. In the context of this study, women's confrontations with family members demonstrate the depth of their desire to make, and the degree of action taken towards making, positive change for themselves.

8
Conclusion

I have depicted women's experiences of emotional abuse as a web in which, as they spiral outward in their movement towards reclaiming their power and towards healing, they free themselves from entanglement. The insidiousness and power of emotional abuse paralleled the invisibility, strength and purpose of a spider's web. Even as women freed themselves from their abusers, they struggled with the elements of their culture which complicated their efforts to separate from abusive partners. These included practical problems presented by being single or the heads of one-parent families, within cultures whose state funding and housing are designed to meet the needs of two-parent families. In addition, the media and popular images of abuse and 'battered women' intensified the vulnerabilities women held as a result of the abuse and impacted women's ability to define their own experiences. Throughout the book I have also identified a number of similarities between abuse or the cultural response to abuse and feminist analysis of women's relation to patriarchal society in general. For example, objectification and sexual degradation as part of emotional abuse echo the issues identified by feminists in their analysis of pornography and media exploitation of women. Also the suppression of women's anger through psychological socialization speaks to women's struggle to acknowledge their anger in making positive, self-protective change in the power dynamics of abuse. Throughout this book the story of women's survival and action for change is also interwoven.

In making the journeys described in this book, women spin a new web, seek a new perspective. They demonstrate an ability to overcome obstacles creatively and find possibilities for new paths. This contrasts dramatically with the images of 'battered women' as helpless, deviant, or pitiful which deny the powerful and creative action women take in their survival of abuse.

The symbolism of this summary is significant. Webs and their creators are potent icons of evil in some cultures, and of wisdom in others. In some native American cultures, for example, the spider is seen as the creator of the alphabet, giving humans the gift of a way to record their journeys through the configurations offered in her web. In some native American cultures, the spider and her web bring the message of continual weaving of life patterns, infinite possibility of creation and the importance of recording the complexities of our life journeys (Sams and Carson, 1988). In somewhat of a parallel, women I interviewed gave me the gift of awareness as to the lack of language available which accurately described their experiences, and a knowledge base upon which to begin building a language. The contributions of their stories and survival could also be likened to a web, one reflecting the wisdom of the spider, which instructs, illuminates and documents rather than one that entraps and victimizes.

In Chapter 6, I spoke of the need for a language which would allow women to express their experiences, particularly with regard to emotional abuse. From the perspective of the women, this need was expressed with regard to confronting the negative responses of others and challenging the inappropriate beliefs about the abuse held by others and portrayed in the media. Thus, a language which conveys the meaning of emotional abuse and its impact is required by women to support their process of leaving abusers. Moreover, development of such an analysis is key to the growth of feminist analysis. Feminist analysis is built on women's experiences, and thus it is essential to have a common language in which women may speak their stories and be understood.

The courage of the women who shared their stories with me provided the basis for this book. This is a step towards such a record and towards creating a new alphabet of concepts and language which can break the silencing of women's lives. The alphabet read from women's webs is translated in this book in a number of ways. First, in Chapter 3 I offer terms to describe emotional abuse and its impact, and thus have begun to establish a framework in which a language could be built which would answer the need described above. Second, I argue that leaving an abuser is a *process* which begins with the women's action to shift the imbalance of power and control, and continues after they leave abusers in terms of how formerly abused women overcome the problems they face. Women's experiences of leaving abusive partners were not that of simple and immediate changes which occurred once they 'decided' to leave. Rather they underwent a process of emotional, material and social struggle which lasted for years. Moreover, this process may include women returning to their partners before they leave them permanently. It extends into the way in which women are confronted with the long-term emotional scars of abuse – the resurgence of fear, anger and low esteem that arose in response to having been abused that occurs repeatedly for long periods after leaving their abusers. The *process* of leaving entails a continual balance between coping with practical problems and utilizing emotional response to fuel change or inform understanding of what has occurred.

The nature of this process is reflected in the recurrence of particular themes throughout my work. Women's experiences were cyclical. They rarely 'left behind' a sense of anger, fear, low esteem, uncertain identity, isolation etc., but confronted these lasting consequences of abuse over and over at different periods in their lives and learned and healed progressively each time a consequence was revisited.

Third, this book informs debate over the use of the term 'victim', which women used to convey their experience of the process of victimization enacted by their partners. This contributes to feminist debates about using the term. Although perhaps inappropriate for explanations of woman abuse, 'victim' may hold specific conceptual meaning for the women who have been abused with regard to the process of change their partners' abuse forced upon them. When women speak of 'feeling like a victim' they may be referring to this process, as were the women I interviewed, rather than labelling themselves.

A final contribution of this work towards creating a language for women and to feminist analysis is the development of the concept 'survival'. In other work on woman abuse the term, until recently, has referred to the coping strategies which enable women to continue functioning in the face of abuse. However, I argue that its use can be extended to reflect the process I have described above. In transforming their past experiences into skills and wisdom for personal and social change, which moves toward overcoming such problems, formerly abused women continue their process of 'survival'.

Additionally, in the light of how the problems women confront compound the impact of abuse, it becomes even more clear why the dimensions of survival discussed in this work are significant. Survival from abuse includes not only recovering from and transforming the wounds incurred from abuse but also confronting those aspects of the culture which actually deepen rather than promote healing of these wounds. When women asserted their needs and perspectives in relationships with others, for example, they were asserting to themselves and those around them that they would not accept the enforcement of others' values or perspectives on them. They were also challenging the acceptance of media representations and the values and beliefs held by significant others which constituted the cultural framework in which their wounds were reinforced. In this way, by effecting change in relationships with those around them and also in the degree of support they provided to other abused women, formerly abused women confront the institutional and cultural structures within which the web of abuse is anchored.

It is these concepts and terminology, as they emerged from the interviews, that represent a step towards creating an alphabet and a language with which we can define the experience of abuse. We weave our own record of our experiences and, in doing so, reclaim the symbolism of the web, reflecting again the transformation of abuse into empowerment.

Appendix 1: Location of and Contact with Interviewees

The British city from which interviewees were drawn is in northern England. Its population is approximately 120,000. One refuge exists in this city, whose services are supported by networks with others in the region. Here I used contacts with a refuge and an organization for single parents. I also wrote a letter to a local paper, requested that a local radio station made calls for volunteers, placed small advertisements in other local newspapers and posted requests for research participants in community centres and public buildings. The latter set of attempts yielded only two participants. The former two sources, however, yielded the remaining nine women. Contact through these organizations was achieved through forwarding letters of introduction via a staff member who upheld the anonymity of the women contacted. My first contact with these women, then, relied on their return of a letter expressing interest in the project and stipulating how I might get in touch with them.

The US city from which interviewees were drawn is on the west coast. It has a population of approximately 8 million in the metropolitan area. Within this and the outlying area, a network of 12 refuges exists. In this city, a small advertisement in a university newspaper uncovered a great deal more interest in the project than I had expected. Unlike my experience with the British newspapers, I found that just a few lines run for three days, under the heading of 'research needs', resulted in 15 responses and 12 actual completed interviews. In order to supplement the diversity of this group of women, I sought to contact more women of colour through the shelter for which I had worked. They put me in contact with five more women, three of whom were women of colour. I also enlisted the aid of a service agency for gays and lesbians which produced the opportunity to interview two lesbian women.

Appendix 2: Data on Women Interviewed

in following categories:

Nationality
US   19
British   11

Type of relationship
Married   18
Living together   10
Dating   2

Number of dependent children
None   11
One   4
Two   9
Three   4
Four   2

Period between leaving partner and interview
One to two years   11
Over two to three years   10
Over three to five years   3
Over five to ten years   2
Over ten years   4

Period in relationship with partner
Less than one year   4
One to three years   7
Over three to five years   7
Over five to ten years   7
Over ten years   5

Ethnicity
White   25
Black   2
Native American   1
Hispanic   2

Refuge usage
Refuge resident   7
Not refuge resident   23

Age in years
17 to 25   7
26 to 35   11

36 to 45	7
46 to 55	4
56 to 65	1

Sexuality

Heterosexual	27
Lesbian	3

Appendix 3: Topic Guide for Interviews

Topic Guide for Interview 1

Personal Background

Age
Employment history
Parents' employment
Ethnicity
Education
Training
Children:
    Ages, sex
    Who do they live with?
    Are they children of abuser?

Abuse

What have you experienced as abusive?
    Mental abuse
    Physical abuse
    Sexual abuse
    Resulting injuries
When and why did the abuse occur?
    First attack
    First seen as abuse
    How often
    Patterns in abuser's behaviour
    Related to substance abuse
    Changes over time and marital status

Reactions to Abuse

Ways tried to stop attacks or abuse:
    Physical
    Verbal or emotional
How successful were attempts?
Feelings about abuse
Feelings about self, changes over time, i.e. guilt, depression, self-image, shame
Feelings about partner, changes over time, i.e. anger, guilt, fear
Children's reactions
Reactions of friends and family
People contacted for help when in relationship
Whom did you tell about abuse?
Service agencies contacted
Responses of service agencies

Outset of Relationship

Age when met partner
Marry? Live together? When, for how long?
Objections to relationship? From whom? Why?
Able to maintain friendships during relationship? Why, why not?
Employed during relationship?
Any financial problems in relationship?

Leaving

Why did you decide to leave?
　Change in feelings
　Specific event or circumstance
Who contacted for help in leaving? People, agencies?
What kind of help asked for?
What responses most helpful?
Use of refuge services: Why, why not, helpful?
Ever return to partner after leaving? Why?
Able to form plans before leaving, concerning: housing, finances?

Additional Notes

Advice to offer women thinking of leaving abusive partners
Changes in services available which would be helpful to women who are trying to leave abusive partners

Topic Guide for Interview 2

Current Situation

How long out of relationship?
Current employment
Better or worse off with regard to: housing, finances, social life, health

Fears

Of ex-partners
Of new partners
Vulnerability to violence in general
Of own feelings and ability to recognize abuse in future

Changes and Coping

Do you, or did you, talk about abuse once you left? To whom? Why? How did listeners respond?
Changes in self-images since left: changes due to being away from abuser or your experience of leaving
Have you changed the way you dress, or look?
In general, feel weaker or stronger as a result of the abuse and experience of leaving?
Are there changes in the future that you would like to see happen?

Changes in Relationships

With parents, siblings

With children
With new partners: tell them about abuse?
Relationships affected by past experience with abuse
Do you think you would ever be abused again?
What would you do?
How would you recognize abuse?
Do you have different expectations of partners?

Thinking about the Past

Do you try to remember, or not remember, the abuse?
What are your feelings when you think about the abuse?
Do you ever have flashbacks? When and why?
Do you ever have nightmares about the abuse?

Attitude Changes

Male and female roles
Marriage/partnerships
Men/women in general
Battered women
Violence:
 In general
 Against women
 In the media

Views about Battered Women

Do you see yourself as 'battered'?
Do you see yourself as a survivor or victim or neither?
Do you feel a commitment to help other abused women?
Have you helped other women?
How has giving that help affected you?
Do you feel any kind of personal bond with other women who have been abused?

Life Changes

Have your priorities changed (i.e. what you feel is most important in your life)?
Changes in philosophies about struggle and abuse
Changes in life direction
Career or educational plans

Additional Notes

Advice for women who have just left abusive partners
Changes in services available to women who have left an abusive partner that would be
 helpful in the long term

Appendix 4: Follow-Up Questions

Dear Participant,

Please fill in this survey a week or two after the second interview. Because you have answered many questions which you may feel are personal or painful and because you have given me hours of your time, I feel it is important for you to express how the interviews might have affected you. It will give me an idea (1) whether the interview allowed you to discuss the experiences you felt were most important to you, and (2) whether you feel the interview has affected your thoughts about abuse. I have not asked you to include your name for the sake of privacy. Please feel free to use the back or enclose additional paper if your response does not fit the space provided. If you have any questions or anything you want to talk to me about, I can be reached at . . . or by post at . . .

1 About how long has it been since your second interview with me? (number of days or weeks)
2 How often, since the second interview, have you thought about either of the interviews in any way? (please tick one)
   . . . Not at all
   . . . Once or twice
   . . . Several times
   . . . Around once a day
   . . . More than once a day
   . . . None of these describe how often I thought about the interview, I would best describe it as . . .
3 Were there any experiences or feelings that you told me about which you have never said to anyone before?
   If so, what was different about the interview situation that allowed you to talk about this?
   How did it feel to tell me this (was it stressful, a relief, or did you have some other feelings about it)?
4 How did you feel, in general, about talking to someone you didn't know about your experiences and feelings (for example, was it uncomfortable, easier etc.)?
   Can you say why this was so?
5 Do you think the interviews have caused you to think about your experience of being abused in any way that is different from the way you felt before? (For example, maybe there has been a change in: how often you think about the abuse, why you think it happened, your feelings about being abused, etc.) Please try to be as specific as possible.
6 If your views have changed, do you think any of these changes occurred because of what I said? Because of what you said? (Is there anything specific that you remember me or you saying that made you think about things differently?)

7 Do you think the interview allowed you to express what you feel is important about your past experience and its effects on you now?

Is there anything you would like to add about what we talked about?

8 Do you have any comments to make about being interviewed by me? (For example, are there other topics which you feel should be brought up by me in future interviews? Were any questions inappropriate or too personal? Was there anything that would have made you feel more at ease about being interviewed? etc.)

References

ADWAS (1992) Training presentation, Abused Deaf Women's Advocacy Services, Seattle, WA.

Ainsworth, M.D.S. (1979) 'Infant–mother attachment', *American Psychologist*, 34: 932–7.

Allen, Paula Gunn (1986) 'Violence and the American Indian woman', in Center for the Prevention of Sexual and Domestic Violence, *The Speaking Profits Us*. Seattle, WA.

Barrett, M. and McIntosh, M. (1982) *The Anti-Social Family*. Norfolk, England: Thetford Press.

Barron, Jackie (1990) *Not Worth the Paper ... ?: the Effectiveness of Legal Protection for Women and Children Experiencing Domestic Violence*. Bristol: Women's Aid Federation, England.

Barry, Kathleen (1979) *Female Sexual Slavery*. New York: Avon.

Beck, Susan Malone, dee Post, Robin and D'Arcy, Genet (1982) 'A study of battered women in a psychiatric setting', *Women and Therapy*, 1 (2): 137–45.

Benowitz, Mindy (1986) 'How homophobia affects lesbians' response to violence in lesbian relationships', in Kerry Lobel (ed.), *Naming the Violence*. Seattle, WA: Seal.

Binney, Val, Harkell, Gina and Nixon, Judy (1981) *Leaving Violent Men: a Study of Refuges and Housing for Battered Women*. National Women's Aid Federation.

Blumer, H. (1969) *Symbolic Interactionism: Perspective and Method*. Englewood Cliffs, NJ: Prentice-Hall.

Bograd, Michelle (1988) 'Feminist perspectives on wife abuse: an introduction', in Kersti Yllö and Michelle Bograd (eds), *Feminist Perspectives on Wife Abuse*. Beverly Hills, CA: Sage.

Bowker, Lee H. (1983) *Beating Wife Beating*. Lexington, MA: Lexington Books, D.C. Heath.

Bowlby, J. (1969) *Attachment and Loss*. New York: Basic Books.

Bowles, Gloria and Klein, Renate Duelli (eds) (1983) *Theories of Women's Studies*. London: Routledge and Kegan Paul.

Branca, Patricia (1975) *Silent Sisterhood*. London: Croom Helm Ltd.

Brienes, Wini and Gordon, Linda (1983) 'The new scholarship on family violence', *Signs*, 8: 490–531.

Brown, Claude (1974) 'The family and the subculture of violence' in Steinmetz and Straus (eds), *Violence in the Family*. New York: Dodd.

Browne, Angela (1987) *When Battered Women Kill*. New York: Free Press.

Brownmiller, Susan (1975) *Against Our Will: Men, Women and Rape*. London: Secker and Warburg.

Bruner, Jerome S., Goodnow, Jacqueline J. and Austin, George A. (1956) *A Study of Thinking*. New York: Wiley.

Burgess, Robert (ed.) (1982) *Field Research: a Sourcebook and Field Manual*. London: Allen and Unwin.

Burgess, Robert (1984) *In the Field: an Introduction to Field Research*. London: Allen and Unwin.

Campbell, Robert N. (1984) *The New Science: Self-Esteem Psychology*. London: University Press of America.

Cantoni, Lucile (1981) 'Clinical issues in domestic violence', *Social Casework*, 62 (1): 3–12.

Center for the Prevention of Sexual and Domestic Violence (1986) *The Speaking Profits Us: Violence in the Lives of Women of Color*. Seattle, WA: Center for the Prevention of Sexual and Domestic Violence.

Chaplin, Jocelyn (1988) *Feminist Counselling in Action*. London: Sage.

Chesler, Phyllis (1972), *Women and Madness*. New York: Avon.

Claerhout, Susan, Elder, John and Janes, Carolyn (1982) 'Problem solving skills of rural battered women', *American Journal of Community Psychology*. 10 (5): 605–12.

Cohen, Arthur (1968) 'Some complications of self-esteem for social influence', in C. Gordon and K. Gergen (eds), *The Self in Social Interaction*. New York: Wiley.

Combahee River Collective (1982) 'A black feminist statement', in Gloria T. Hull, Patricia Bell Scott and Barbara Smith (eds), *But Some of Us are Brave*. New York: Feminist Press.

Courtois, Christine A. (1988) *Healing the Incest Wound: Adult Survivors in Therapy.* London: W.W. Norton.

Delphy, Christine and Leonard, Diana (1992) *Familiar Exploitation*. Cambridge: Polity.

Dobash, R.E. and Dobash, R.P. (1978) 'Wives: the appropriate victims of marital violence', *Victimology*. 2 (3–4): 426–42.

Dobash, R.E. and Dobash, R.P. (1980) *Violence against Wives: a Case against the Patriarchy*. London: Open Books.

Dobash, R.E. and Dobash, R.P. (1981) 'Community response to violence against wives: charivari, abstract justice and patriarchy', *Social Problems*. 28 (5): 563–81.

Dobash, R.E. and Dobash, R.P. (1988) 'Research as social action: the struggle for battered women', in Kersti Yllö and Michelle Bograd (eds), *Feminist Perspectives on Wife Abuse*. Beverly Hills, CA: Sage.

Dobash, R.E. and Dobash, R.P. (1992) *Women, Violence and Social Change*. London: Routledge and Kegan Paul.

Durkheim, E. (1984) *The Division of Labor in Society*. New York: Free Press.

Dworkin, Andrea (1981) *Pornography: Men Possessing Women*. London: Women's Press.

Dworkin, Andrea (1987) *Intercourse*. London: Secker and Warburg.

Edgington, Amy (1988) 'Lesbian battering conference', *Off Our Backs*, November: 8–9, 21.

Edwards, Anne (1987) 'Male violence in feminist theory', in Jalna Hanmer and Mary Maynard (eds), *Women, Violence and Social Control*. London: Macmillan.

Edwards, Susan S.M. (1987) 'Provoking her own demise: from common assault to homicide', in Jalna Hanmer and Mary Maynard (eds), *Women, Violence and Social Control*. London: Macmillan Press.

Edwards, Susan S.M. (1989) *Policing Domestic Violence: Women, the Law and the State*. London: Sage.

Egan, Gerard (1982) *The Skilled Helper*. Monterey, CA: Brooks/Cole.

Eichenbaum, Luise and Orbach, Susie (1985) *Understanding Women*. London: Pelican.

Etzioni, Amitai (1968) *The Active Society*. London: Collier-Macmillan.

Ferraro, Kathleen J. (1979) 'Physical and emotional battering: aspects of managing hurt', *California Sociologist*, 2 (2): 134–49.

Ferraro, Kathleen J. (1983) 'Rationalizing violence: how battered women stay', *Victimology*, 8 (3–4): 203–12

Ferraro, K.J. and Johnson, J.M. (1983) 'How women experience battering: the process of victimization', *Social Problems*, 30 (3): 326–39.

Finch, Janet (1984) ' "It's great to have someone to talk to": the ethics and politics of interviewing women', in Colin Bell and H. Roberts (eds), *Social Researching*. London: Routledge and Kegan Paul.

Finn, Jerry (1985) 'The stresses and coping behaviour of battered women', *Social Casework*, 66 (6): 341–9.

Foote, Nelson (1951) 'Identification as the basis for a theory of motivation', *American Sociological Review*, 16: 14–21.

Freidan, Betty (1963) *The Feminine Mystique*. New York: Dell.

Friedman, Raymond (1974) 'The psychology of depression: an overview' in R. Friedman and J. Katz (eds), *The Psychology of Depression: Contemporary Theory and Research*. Washington, DC: V.H. Winston.

Frye, Marilyn (1983) *The Politics of Reality: Essays in Feminist Theory*. New York: Crossing Press.

Gayford, J.J. (1975) 'Wife battering: a preliminary survey of 100 cases', *British Medical Journal*, 25 (January): 194–7.

Gayford, J.J. (1976) 'Ten types of battered wives', *The Welfare Officer*, 1 (January): 5–9.

Gelles, Richard J. (1974) *The Violent Home: a Study of Physical Aggression between Husbands and Wives*. Beverly Hills, CA: Sage.

Gelles, Richard J. (1976) 'Abused wives: why do they stay?', *Journal of Marriage and the Family*, 38 (4): 659–68.

Gelles, Richard J. (1979) *Family Violence*. Beverly Hills, CA: Sage.

Gelles, Richard and Straus, Murray (1988) *Intimate Violence: the Definitive Study of the Causes and Consequences of Abuse in the American Family*. New York: Simon and Schuster.

Gibbs, Jack P. (1989) *Control: Sociology's Central Notion*. Urbana: University of Illinois Press.

Gilbert, Paul (1984) *Depression: from Psychology to Brain State*. London: Lawrence Erlbaum.

Gilligan, Carol (1982) *In a Different Voice*. Cambridge, MA: Harvard University Press.

Gittins, D. (1985) *The Family in Question*. London: Macmillan.

Glaser, Barney and Strauss, Anselm L. (1967) *The Discovery of Grounded Theory: Strategies for Qualitative Research*. Chicago: Aldine.

Gordon, Linda (1986) 'Family violence, feminism and social control', *Feminist Studies*, 12 (3): 453–78.

Graham, Hilary (1984) 'Surviving through stories', in Colin Bell and H. Roberts (eds), *Social Researching*. London: Routledge and Kegan Paul.

Graham, Hilary (1986) 'Do her answers fit his questions? Women and the survey method', in E. Gamarnikow et al., *The Public and the Private*. Hampshire: Gower.

Griffin, Susan (1971) 'Rape: the all American crime', in *The Politics of Rape*. New York: Harper and Row.

Griffin, Susan (1981) *Pornography and Silence*. New York: Harper and Row.

Hammond, Nancy (1986) 'Lesbians and the reluctance to identify abuse', in Kerry Lobel (ed.), *Naming the Violence*. Seattle, WA: Seal.

Hanmer, Jalna (1978) 'Violence and the social control of women', in Garry Littlejohn, Barry Smart, John Wakeford and Nira Yuval-Davis (eds), *Power and the State*. London: Croom Helm.

Hanmer, Jalna (1988) 'Women, violence and crime prevention'. Paper presented at the University of York Staff Graduate Seminar, 12 May 1988.

Hanmer, Jalna and Maynard, Mary (eds) (1987) *Women, Violence and Social Control.* London: Macmillan.

Hanmer, Jalna and Saunders, Sheila (1984) *Well Founded Fear.* London: Hutchinson.

Hanmer, Jalna and Saunders, Sheila (1986) 'Blowing the cover on the protective male: a community study of violence to women', in Eva Gamarnikow, David Morgan, June Pervis and Daphne Taylorson (eds), *The Public and the Private.* Hampshire: Gower.

Harding, S. (1981) 'Is there a feminist method?' in S. Harding (ed.), *Feminism and Methodology.* Milton Keynes: Open University Press.

Harding, S. (1986) *The Science Question in Feminism.* Ithaca, RI: Cornell University Press.

Hart, Barbara (1986) 'Preface' and 'Lesbian battering: an examination', in Kerry Lobel (ed.), *Naming the Violence.* Seattle, WA: Seal.

Hart, Barbara (1988) 'Violence in lesbian relationships: a discussion paper'. Material for the Lesbian Task Force of the NCADV conference on 8 June 1988.

Hawley, Amos H. (1963) 'Community poor and urban renewal success', *The American Journal of Sociology*, 68, January: 422–31.

Hoff, Lee Ann (1990) *Battered Women as Survivors.* London: Routledge.

Homer, Margorie, Leonard, Anne and Homer, Pat Taylor (1984) *Private Violence: Public Shame.* Cleveland: Cleveland Refuge and Aid for Women and Children.

Homer, Margorie, Leonard, Anne and Homer, Pat Taylor (1985) 'Personal relationships: help or hindrance', in N. Johnson (ed.), *Marital Violence.* London: Routledge and Kegan Paul.

Hooks, Bell (1984) *Feminist Theory: From Margin to Center.* Boston, MA: South End Press.

Hooper, Carol-Ann (1991) *Mothers Surviving Child Sexual Abuse.* London: Tavistock/ Routledge and Kegan Paul.

Hornung, C.A., McCullough, B.C. and Sugimoto, T. (1981) 'Status relationships in marriage: risk factors in spouse abuse', *Journal of Marriage and the Family*, 43 (3): 675–92.

Hull, Gloria T., Scott, Patricia Bell and Smith, Barbara (eds) (1982) *All the Women are White, all the Blacks are Men, But Some of Us are Brave.* New York: Feminist Press.

Hunt, J. (1965) 'Intrinsic motivation and its role in psychological development', in D. Levine (ed.), *Nebraska Symposium on Motivation.* 13. Lincoln: University of Nebraska Press.

Jackson, Stevi and Rushton, Peter (1982) 'Victims and villains: images of women in accounts of family violence', *Women's Studies International Forum* 5 (1): 17–28.

James, William (1910) *The Principles of Psychology.* London: Macmillan.

Johnson, Miriam (1989) 'Feminism and the theories of Talcott Parsons', in Ruth Wallace (ed.), *Feminism and Sociological Theory.* London: Sage.

Johnson, Norman (ed.) (1985) *Marital Violence.* London: Routledge and Kegan Paul.

Kalmusst, Debra S. and Straus, Murray A. (1982) 'Wives' marital dependency and wife abuse', *Journal of Marriage and the Family*, 44 (2): 277–86.

KALX Radio (1985) 'Domestic violence by and against women: an interview about lesbian violence'. KALX, Berkeley, CA.

Kaplan, H.B. (1975) *Self-attitudes and Deviant Behaviour.* Pacific Palisades, NJ: Goodyear.

Keller, Evelyn Fox (1985) *Reflections on Gender and Science.* Yale: Yale University Press.

Kelly, Liz (1987) 'The continuum of sexual violence', in Jalna Hanmer and Mary Maynard (eds), *Women, Violence and Social Control.* London: Macmillan.

Kelly, Liz (1988a) 'How women define their experiences of violence', in Kersti Yllö and

Michelle Bograd (eds), *Feminist Perspectives on Wife Abuse*. Beverly Hills, CA: Sage.

Kelly, Liz (1988b) *Surviving Sexual Violence*. Cambridge: Polity.

Kelly, Liz (1991) 'Unspeakable acts: women who abuse', *Trouble and Strife*, 21: 13–20.

Kelly, Liz, Scott, Sarah and Bell, Ellen (1989) 'With our own hands', *Trouble and Strife*, 16 (Summer): 26–8.

Kenney, Catherine (1989) *Counselling the Survivors of Sexual Abuse*. Norwich: Social Work Monographs.

Koslof, Karen E. (1984) 'The battered women: a development perspective', *Smith College Studies in Social Work*, 54 (3): 181–203.

Lather, Pattie (1988) 'Feminist perspectives on empowering research methodologies', *Women's Studies International Forum*, 11: 569–81.

Laws, S. (1986) 'The social meaning of menstruation: a feminist investigation'. PhD thesis, Warwick University.

Lerner, Harriet Goldhor (1990) *The Dance of Anger*. New York: Harper and Row.

Lion, John R. (1977) 'Clinical aspects of wife battering', in Maria Roy (ed.), *Battered Women*. New York: Van Nostrand Reinhold.

Lobel, Kerry (ed.) (1986) *Naming the Violence: Speaking Out about Lesbian Violence*. Seattle, WA: Seal.

Loseke, Donileen R. and Cahill, Spencer E. (1984) 'The social construction of deviance: experts on battered women', *Social Problems*, 30 (3): 296–310.

Lukes, Steven (1976) *Power: a Radical View*. London: Macmillan.

Mama, Amina (1989a) 'Violence against black women: gender, race and state responses', *Feminist Review*, 32 (Summer): 30–48.

Mama, Amina (1989b) *The Hidden Struggle: Statutory and Voluntary Sector Responses to Violence against Black Women in the Home*. London: London Race and Housing Unit.

Manis, J.G. and Meltzer, B.N. (1972) *Symbolic Interactionism*. Boston: Allyn Bacon.

Mann, Bonnie (1987) 'Working with battered women: radical education or therapy', in *In Our Best Interest: a Process for Personal and Social Change*. MN: Minnesota Program Development.

Marin, E.A. (1985) 'A heap of broken images: a field study and analysis of the long term effects of battering on women in the northwest of England'. MA thesis, Keele University.

Marsden, Dennis and Owens, David (1975) 'Jekyl and Hyde marriages', *New Society*, 32 (8 May): 333–5.

Martin, D. (1976) *Battered Wives*. New York: Pocket Books.

Martin, D. (1978) 'Battered women: society's problem', in Jane Chapman and Margaret Gates (eds), *The Victimization of Women*. Beverly Hills, CA: Sage.

Martin, Roderick (1977) *The Sociology of Power*. London: Routledge and Kegan Paul.

Maslow, A. (1962) *Toward a Psychology of Being*. Princeton, NJ: Van Nostrand.

Mazzola, Donna-Marie (1987) 'The battered women's movement in 19th and 20th century Britain'. Master's thesis, University of York, England, Centre for Women's Studies.

McCall, George and Simmons, J.L. (1966) *Identities and Interactions*. New York: Free Press.

McKinnon, Catherine (1992) Interview with *Time* Magazine, 30 March.

McShane, Claudette (1988) *Warning! Dating may be Hazardous to your Health*. Racine, WI: Mother Courage Press.

Mead, George H. (1962) *Mind, Self and Society*. Chicago: University of Chicago Press.

Mendels, Joseph (1970) *Concepts of Depression*. London: Wiley.

Mies, Maria (1983) 'Towards a methodology for feminist research', in G. Bowles and R. Duelli Klein (eds), *Theories of Women's Studies*. London: Routledge and Kegan Paul.

Millman, Marcia (1975) 'She did it all for love: a feminist view of the sociology of deviance', in M. Millman and R. Kanter (eds), *Another Voice*. New York: Anchor Books.

Morgan, Patricia A. (1981) 'From battered wife to program client: the state's shaping of social problems', *Kapitalistate*, 9: 17–40.

Ms (1989). April.

Nelson, Sarah (1987) *Incest: Fact and Myth*. Edinburgh: Stramullion Cooperative.

Newsweek (1988). 12 December.

NiCarthy, Ginny (1986) *Getting Free: a Handbook for Women in Abusive Relationships*. Seattle, WA: Seal.

NiCarthy, Ginny (1987) *The Ones Who Got Away: Women who Left Abusive Partners*. Seattle, WA: Seal.

NWAF (1977) *Battered Women Need Refuges*. Pamphlet, National Women's Aid Federation.

NWAF (1979) *Battered Women, Refuges and Women's Aid: A Report from the NWAF*. National Women's Aid Federation.

NWIRP (Northwest Immigrant Rights Project) (1992) 'What is conditional permanent residence?', Flyer. Seattle, WA: NWIRP.

Oakley, A. (1981) 'Interviewing women: a contradition in terms', in H. Roberts (ed.), *Doing Feminist Research*. London: Routledge and Kegan Paul.

O'Brien, John E. (1974) 'Violence in divorce-prone families', in Susan K. Steinmetz and Murray Straus (eds), *Violence in the Family*. New York: Dodd.

Olsen, Marvin (1970) *Power in Societies*. New York: Macmillan.

Pagelow, Mildred Daley (1981a) *Woman Battering: Victims and their Experiences*. Beverly Hills, CA: Sage.

Pagelow, Mildred Daley (1981b) 'Factors affecting women's decisions to leave violent relationships', *Journal of Family Issues*, 2 (4): 391–414.

Pahl, Jan (1978) *A Refuge for Battered Women: a Study of the Role of a Women's Centre*. London: HMSO.

Pahl, Jan (1985a) 'Refuges for battered women: ideology and action', *Feminist Review* 19 (March): 25–43.

Pahl, Jan (1985b) *Private Violence and Public Policy: the Needs of Battered Women and the Response of the Public Services*. London: Routledge and Kegan Paul.

Pharr, Suzanne (1988) *Homophobia: a Weapon of Sexism*. Little Rock, AR: Chardon.

Piaget, J. and Inhelder (1969) *The Psychology of the Child*. New York: Basic Books.

Pizzey, Erin (1974) *Scream Quietly or the Neighbours Will Hear*. Harmondsworth: Penguin.

Pizzey, Erin and Shapiro, Jeff (1981) 'Choosing a violent relationship', *New Society*, 23 April: 133–5.

Pleck, Elizabeth (1987) *Domestic Tyranny: the Making of Social Policy against Family Violence from Colonial Times to the Present*. Oxford: Oxford University Press.

Prescott, Suzanne and Letko, Carolyn (1977) 'Battered women: a social psychological perspective', in Maria Roy (ed.), *Battered Women*. New York: Van Nostrand Reinhold.

Ptacek, James (1988) 'Why do men batter their wives?', in Kersti Yllö and Michelle Bograd (eds), *Feminist Perspectives on Wife Abuse*. Beverly Hills, CA: Sage.

Radford, Jill and Kelly, Liz (1991) 'Change the law 2', *Trouble and Strife*, 22.

Ramazanoglu, Caroline (1989) 'Improving on sociology: the problems of taking a feminist standpoint', *Sociology*, 23 (32).

Richardson, Laural and Taylor, Verta (eds) (1983) *Feminist Frontiers: Rethinking Sex, Gender and Society*. Reading, MA: Addison-Wesley.

Roberts, H. (1981) *Doing Feminist Research*. London: Routledge and Kegan Paul.

Romero, Mary (1985) 'A comparison between strategies used on prisoners of war and battered wives', *Sex Roles*, 13 (9–10): 537–47.

Rowe, Dorothy (1978) *Battered Women: a Psychosocial Study of Domestic Violence*. New York: Van Nostrand Reinhold.

Roy, Maria (ed.) (1977) *Battered Women*. New York: Litton Educational.

Russell, Diana (1982) *Rape in Marriage*. New York: Macmillan.

RTIC (1992) Proposition Two, *Responding to Domestic Violence: a Co-ordinated Approach*. Regional Training Implementation Committee. King County Women's Program, Seattle, WA.

Sams, J. and Carson, D. (1988) *Medicine Cards: the Discovery of Power through the Ways of the Animals*. Santa Fe, NM: Bear.

Saunders, Daniel G. (1988) 'Wife abuse, husband abuse or mutual combat?: a feminist perspective on the empirical findings', in Kersti Yllö and Michelle Bograd (eds), *Feminist Perspectives on Wife Abuse*, Beverly Hills, CA: Sage.

Schechter, Susan (1982) *Women and Male Violence*. Boston, MA: South End Press.

Schlessinger, Phillip, Dobash, R.E. and Dobash, Russell (1992) *Women Viewing Violence*. London: British Film Institute.

Scott, P.D. (1974) 'Battered wives', *British Journal of Psychiatry*, 125 (November): 433–41.

Scott, S. (1984) 'The personable and the powerful: gender and status in sociological research', in Colin Bell and H. Roberts (eds), *Social Researching: Politics, Problems and Practice*. London: Routledge and Kegan Paul.

Segal, Lynne (ed.) (1983) *What is to be Done about the Family?* Middlesex: Penguin.

Shainess, Natalie (1977) 'Psychological aspects of wife battering', in Maria Roy (ed.), *Battered Women*. New York: Van Nostrand Reinhold.

Snell, J., Rosenwald, R. and Robey, A. (1964) 'The Wife Beater's Wife', *Archives of General Psychiatry*, 11 (August): 107–12.

Southall Black Sisters (1990) *Against the Grain: a Celebration of Survival and Struggle*.

Spencer (1987) *Principles of Sociology*. New York: Appleton.

Spender, Dale (ed.) (1981) *Men's Studies Modified: the Impact of Feminism on the Academic Disciplines*. Oxford: Pergamon.

Stanko, E. (1985) *Intimate Intrusions: Women's Experience of Male Violence*. London: Routledge and Kegan Paul.

Stanko, E. (1987) 'Typical violence, normal precaution: men, women and interpersonal violence in England, Wales, Scotland and the USA', in Jalna Hanmer and Mary Maynard (eds), *Women, Violence and Social Control*. London: Macmillan.

Stanley, Liz (ed.) (1990) *Feminist Praxis*. London: Routledge.

Stanley, Liz and Wise, Sue (1979) 'Feminist research, feminist consciousness and experiences of sexism', *Women's Studies International Quarterly*, 2 (3): 359–74.

Stanley, Liz and Wise, Sue (1983a) *Breaking Out: Feminist Consciousness and Feminist Research*. London: Routledge and Kegan Paul.

Stanley, Liz and Wise, Sue (1983b) ' "Back to the personal" or: our attempt to construct "feminist research" ', in G. Bowles and R. Duelli Klein (eds), *Theories of Women's Studies*. London: Routledge and Kegan Paul.

Stark, Evan, Flitcraft, Ann and Frazier, William (1979) 'Medicine and patriarchal violence', *International Journal of Health Services*, 9 (3): 461–93.

Stark, Evan, Flitcraft, Ann and Frazier, William (1982) 'Medical therapy as repression: the case of the battered woman', *Health and Medicine*, Summer/Fall: 29–32.

Stark, Rodney and McEvoy III, James (1970) 'Middle class violence', *Psychology Today* 4 (November): 52–65.

Steinmetz, Suzanne and Straus, Murray (eds) (1974) *Violence in the Family*. New York: Dodd.

Steinmetz, Suzanne (ed.) (1977a) *The Cycle of Violence*. New York: Praeger.

Steinmetz, Suzanne (1977b) 'Wife beating, husband beating – a comparison of the use of physical violence between spouses to resolve marital fights' in Maria Roy (ed.), *Battered Women*. NY: Litton Educational.

Straus, Murray A. (1980) 'A sociological perspective on the causes of family violence' in Green (ed.), *Violence in the Family*. Boulder, CO: Westview.

Straus, Murray A., Gelles, Richard and Steinmetz, Suzanne K. (1980) *Behind Closed Doors: Violence in the American Family*. New York: Doubleday.

Strauss, A. (1959) *Mirrors and Masks: the Search for Identity*. Glencoe, II: Free Press.

Sutton, Jo (1979) 'Modern and Victorian battered women: a new look at an old pattern', in *Battered Women and Abused Children*, University of Bradford, England, Issues Occasional Paper 4.

Turner, Janine (1984) *A Crying Game: Diary of a Battered Wife*. Edinburgh: Mainstream Publishing.

University of Bradford (1979) *Battered Women and Abused Children*, University of Bradford, England, Issues Occasional Paper 4.

WAFE (1979) *Battered Women, Refuges and Women's Aid: a Report from the NWAF*. Pamphlet, Women's Aid Federation, England.

WAFE (1990) Report in *Trouble and Strife*, 16.

Waites, Elizabeth (1977) 'Female masochism and the enforced restriction of choice', *Victimology*, 2 (3–4): 535–44.

Walker, Lenore E. (1979a) *The Battered Woman*. New York: Harper and Row.

Walker, Lenore E. (1979b) 'How battering happens and how to stop it', in Donna Moore (ed.), *Battered Women*. Beverly Hills, CA: Sage.

Walker, Lenore E. (1984) *The Battered Woman Syndrome*. New York: Springer.

Warren, Carol A.B. (1988) *Gender Issues in Field Research*. London: Sage.

Weitzman, Jack and Dreen, Karen (1982) 'Wife beating: a view of the marital dyad', *Social Casework*, 63 (5): 259–65.

Welsh Women's Aid (1980) *Mrs Hobson's Choice: a Survey of the Unemployment Position of Women who have been through Women's Aid Refuges in South Wales*. Welsh Women's Aid Research Group.

Westen, Drew (1985) *Self and Society*. London: Cambridge University Press.

White, Evelyn C. (1985) *Chain Chain Change: for Black Women Dealing with Physical and Emotional Abuse*. Seattle, WA: Seal.

White, Evelyn C. (1986) 'Life is a song worth singing: ending violence in the black family', in *The Speaking Profits Us*. Center for the Prevention of Sexual and Domestic Violence, Seattle, WA.

Whyte, William Foote (1982) 'Interviewing in the field', in Robert Burgess (ed.), *Field Research: a Sourcebook and Field Manual*. London: Allen and Unwin.

Women's Research Centre (1989) *Recollecting our Lives: Women's Experience of Child Sexual Abuse*. Vancouver: Press Gang.

Wylie, Ruth (1961) *The Self Concept*. Lincoln: University of Nebraska Press.

Yllö, Kersti (1984) 'The status of women, marital equality and violence against wives: a contextual analysis', *Journal of Family Issues*, 5 (3): 307–20.

Yllö, Kersti (1988) 'Political and methodological debates in wife abuse research'. in Yllö and Bograd (eds) *Feminist Perspectives on Wife Abuse*. Beverly Hills, CA: Sage.

Yllö, Kersti, and Bograd, Michelle (1988) *Feminist Perspectives on Wife Abuse.* Beverly Hills, CA: Sage.

Zambrano, Myrna M. (1985) *Mejor sola Que Mal Acompanada: For the Latina in an Abusive Relationship.* Seattle, WA: Seal.

Index